THE NEW MERMAIDS

Edward the Second

THE NEW MERMAIDS

General Editors
PHILIP BROCKBANK
Professor of English, University of York

BRIAN MORRIS
Professor of English, University of Sheffield

Edward the Second

CHRISTOPHER MARLOWE

Edited by W. MOELWYN MERCHANT

ERNEST BENN LIMITED
LONDON

First published in this form 1967
by Ernest Benn Limited
25 New Street Square . Fleet Street . London . EC4A 3JA
Second impression 1972
© *Ernest Benn Limited 1967*
Distributed in Canada by
The General Publishing Company Limited . Toronto
Printed in Great Britain
ISBN 0 510-33806-2 *Paperback*

CONTENTS

Acknowledgements   vii

Introduction   ix

    The Author   ix

    Date and Source   xi

    The Play   xiv

Note on the Text   xxvii

Further Reading   xxix

The Illustrations   xxx

EDWARD THE SECOND   1

    Dramatis Personae   5

    The Text   7

ACKNOWLEDGEMENTS

THE WORKS of Christopher Marlowe in general and *Edward the Second* in particular have received distinguished editing in the past and any editor to-day will be indebted to the former editions of Robinson (1826), Dyce (1850 and 1858), Cunningham (1870), Fleay (1877), Bullen (1885), Tucker Brooke (1910) and W. D. Briggs (1914). Acknowledgment must also be made of the useful and elaborate apparatus in W. Wagner's edition (Hamburg, 1871) and to the predecessor of this present edition, Havelock Ellis's Mermaid edition (1887). Greater and more immediate debts are owed to W. W. Greg's *Malone Society Reprint* of the 1594 quarto and to the Methuen edition of the *Complete Works* (General Editor R. H. Case) in which *Edward the Second* was edited by H. B. Charlton and R. D. Waller (1933) and revised by F. N. Lees (1955). My detailed dependence on other scholars and critics will be clear from the Introduction and Notes and more briefly indicated under Further Reading. I am grateful to the library staffs of the British Museum, the Victoria and Albert Museum and the University of Exeter for their many courtesies and to my colleagues in the English research seminar of this university for their help and encouragement.

INTRODUCTION

THE AUTHOR

FEW AUTHORS and certainly very few dramatists have suffered more than Christopher Marlowe from a tendentious interpretation of the relation between his life and writings. His violent end, as he 'died swearing' in ambiguous circumstances, has been read back into the matter of his very brief creative life. It is certainly expedient to reconsider the facts of his life objectively and to make critical relationships only when they are strictly relevant.

John Marlowe, shoemaker and freeman of the city of Canterbury, married, in 1561 in the church of St. George the Martyr, Catherine Arthur, who was probably the daughter of the Reverend Christopher Arthur, rector of St. Peter's, Canterbury. Their son was baptised in St. George's in 1564, the register containing the following entry:

> The 26th day of ffebruary was Christened Christofer the sonne of John Marlow.

He was therefore older by some two months than his contemporary Shakespeare and born into a family of very similar avocation, standing and influence. Marlowe's family appears to have prospered during his childhood and youth and his father became in 1585 parish clerk in the parish of St. Mary Bredman.

Christopher Marlowe entered the King's School on 14 January 1579 and nearly two years later, in December 1580, went to Corpus Christi College, Cambridge on a scholarship founded by Archbishop Parker for scholars of the King's School. He graduated B.A. in 1584 and proceeded to the M.A. in 1587. At about this time *Tamburlaine* was acted by the Lord Admiral's Men. But already we are faced with ambiguities concerning his life and opinions.

Under the terms of the Parker Scholarship the scholars were to receive their stipends for six years if it was their intention to take holy orders and for three years if it was not their intention. The four scholars who shared rooms with Marlowe in Corpus Christi College, Lewgar, Thexton, Munday and Cockman, 'all became apparently exemplary clergymen and lived long lives' (Tucker Brooke) and it seems clear that Marlowe had also satisfied the university authorities of his intention to be ordained. At the same time there seems to have been some doubt concerning his proceeding to the M.A. in 1587, for on 29 June the Privy Council wrote to the university:

> Whereas it was reported that Christopher Morley was determined to have gone beyond the seas to Rheims and there to remain [i.e. to become a seminarist at Rheims], their Lordships thought good to certify that he had no such intent, but that in all his actions he had behaved himself orderly and discreetly, whereby he had done her Majesty good service . . . Their Lordships' request was that the rumour thereof should be allayed by all possible means and that he should be furthered in the degree he was to take this next Commencement [i.e. M.A. in 1587].

It would seem therefore that this young scholar was sufficiently respected by the Privy Council to be entrusted by them to undertake services abroad perhaps as recently as the period between March and June 1587, the dates of his supplication for the M.A. and the Privy Council letter to the University; and that this visit to the continent had brought him under suspicion of Roman Catholic leanings. He can, at his age and with his experience, have been no very distinguished emissary of the Privy Council, but among those who caused the letter to be sent to the University of Cambridge were Archbishop Whitgift, Sir Christopher Hatton (the Lord Chancellor) and Lord Burghley (the Lord Treasurer), shrewd and careful men at a time when national affairs were confused and dangerous.

Most of the remaining brief five years of his life were spent, with little public stir or note, in London or at Scadbury, the home of Sir Thomas Walsingham near Chislehurst in Kent. These obscure years saw the writing—or completion—of seven plays and a considerable body of poetry which included *Hero and Leander*, the translation of the first book of Lucan's *Pharsalia* and *All Ouids Elegies: 3 Bookes*. His known friends during this time of swift creativity included Sir Walter Raleigh, Thomas Nashe and George Chapman; the mathematician Thomas Hariot belonged to the group who earned for Marlowe, Raleigh and Chapman the reputation of daring intellectual exploration, a reputation which an uneasy companionship with Kyd confirmed; for the latter found it expedient to write to Sir John Puckering, a member of the Privy Council, soon after Marlowe's death in 1593 in terms which served to exonerate him from culpable association with Marlowe: though Kyd admits that they were 'wrytinge in our chamber twoe yeares synce . . . that I shold loue or be familer frend, with one so irreligious, were verie rare . . . [for] he was intemperate and of a cruel hart, the verie contraries to which, my greatest enemies will saie by me'. His reason for writing to Puckering was 'to cleere my self of being thought an Atheist, which some will swear he was'. This charge is examined admirably and in detail by Paul Kocher (see Further Reading) and it is unnecessary here to do more than summarise the charges with which one Richard Baines reinforced the implications of Kyd's letters. Tucker Brooke (who reprints the whole document) characterises the bulk of the statements attributed to Marlowe as 'critical observations, likely enough to have been uttered in the course of argument by an imprudent man interested in the philosophy of religion'. One might add that there is a constant tone of deliberate provocation in the statements which squares with the sense of rashness in word and action apparently characteristic of Marlowe:

. . . That the first beginning of religion was only to keep men in awe.

. . . That Christ was a bastard and his mother dishonest.

. . . That if he were put to write a new religion, he would undertake both a more excellent and admirable method and that all the new testament is filthily written [presumably in unclassical Greek].

This union of rash speculation and a desire to flaunt opinions in the face of puritan zeal was dangerous to Marlowe and his intellectual associates; at the same time it masked a true gravity in Marlowe's thinking which we shall find issuing in some of the themes of *Edward the Second*. This was a lively, precocious and recalcitrant intelligence, skirmishing in and out of religious, social and political orthodoxy.

The drama of Marlowe's dying in an inn brawl at Deptford on 30 May has focused too much curiosity, throwing a retrospective quality of violence over his brief literary and intellectual life. The known facts are simple. On 12 May Kyd was arrested and questioned under torture concerning treasonable and heretical opinions. On 18 May the Privy Council issued a warrant for Marlowe's arrest and he was taken on 20 May at Walsingham's home and required to give daily attendance until 'licensed to the contrary'. On 30 May he was stabbed by Frizer, allegedly in self-defence in a quarrel over a disputed reckoning—and more detail scarcely concerns the critic of the play. He died young, may have 'died swearing', may have had dubious companions in 'espionage' but all this probably belongs more firmly with literary gossip than with criticism.

DATE AND SOURCE

The earliest entry concerning *Edward the Second* in the Stationers' Register reads:

vj^{to} Iulij [1593]
Entred for his copie vnder thandes of Master Richard Iudson
and the Wardens./A booke. Intituled The troublesom Reign and
Lamentable Death of Edward the Second, king of England, with
the tragicall fall of proud Mortymer

This was entered for 'William Iones' and the earliest extant copy of
the play was published by William Jones in the following year with
the title:

The troublesome/raigne and lamentable death of/Edward *the second,*
King of/England: with the tragicall/*fall of proud* Mortimer:

to which was added in 1598 and subsequent editions:

And also the life and death of *Peirs Gaueston,*/*the great Earle of*
Cornewall, *and mighty*/fauorite of king *Edward* the second, as it
was/*publiquely acted by the right honorable*/*the Earle of Pembrooke*
his/*seruantes.*

All these editions agree in the attribution:

Written by Chri. Marlow *Gent.*

It was thus entered and published very soon after Marlowe's death
and most critics are agreed that it was among the latest and most
mature of his plays, though J. C. Maxwell found it questionable
whether 'his last play was *Faustus* or the relatively lifeless and derivative *Edward II*' and others have agreed with this chronological
implication but without the critical judgment added.

The description of the play as derivative raises the further
question of dating in relation to Shakespeare's second and third parts
of *King Henry the Sixth* and to the anonymous manuscript play,
Thomas of Woodstock (edited by A. P. Rossiter, 1946). Whereas
Marlowe was formerly considered a Shakespearian forerunner, it is
now generally agreed that Marlowe's *Edward the Second* followed
both the early Shakespeare history plays and the low-keyed *Woodstock.* Large numbers of parallel passages in these plays (and some
others, including *Arden of Feversham* and Peele's *Edward the First*)
have been cited, from which precise chronological dependence is
impossible to determine with certainty nor is it of ultimate critical
significance. It is now more important to place Marlowe's muted
interest in historical event and to discriminate carefully his role in
the development of the history play in the Elizabethan theatre—a
genre which has too often been regarded as homogeneous and a
repository of generally held commonplaces. Neither Shakespeare
nor Marlowe are patient of this summary treatment, nor have they
themselves wholly congruous aims in their 'historical' writing.

The sources of the play and their manipulation have therefore some importance. The immediate source for the main matter of the play is Holinshed's *Chronicles of England* (first published in 1577) but the twenty-three years of historical time are dramatically compressed to a swift narrative sequence, the ambiguities of which are well summarised by Charlton and Waller (edition of 1933): 'According to a strict analysis the action could be compassed within a year, in which Edward lost wife, crown, and life; the impression on the mind is both one of rapid development and of the passage of considerable time'. Marlowe went to two other sources for details of Edward's terrible death. His humiliation by Matrevis and Gurney, his shaving in cold puddle water before his imprisonment, seems to have been taken from Stow's *Annales* (published in 1592; 'devising to disfigure him that he might not be known'), while the 'Maidens of England' jig in Act II is probably from Fabyan's *Chronicle* (published in 1533). We have had recently a suggested source for Lightborn, Edward's executioner, which goes behind the chronicle material. Harry Levin (*Christopher Marlowe: The Overreacher*, 1954) takes 'Lightborn' to be a translation of 'Lucifer', a suggestive relation of Edward's death to the mediaeval tortures of the damned, which we shall look at later in this introduction.

Unlike the other plays of Marlowe, the text of *Edward the Second* is sound and well authenticated (see Note on the Text, p. xxvii). Its stage presentation however is ambiguous and sporadic. The early title pages refer to the Earl of Pembroke's company and they may have presented it, in the provinces or London, in the closing months of 1592. Later editions, including that published by Roger Barnes in 1612, continue to mention the Pembroke company, until the 1622 quarto published by Henry Bell, 'As it was publikely Acted by the late Queenes Maiesties Seruants at the Red Bull in S. Iohns streete', an open theatre like the Globe, built about 1604 in Clerkenwell.

After these productions in the Jacobean theatre it seems to have been little seen until its revival in this century, first by William Poel in 1903 and subsequently in a number of academic productions. The Marlowe Society did not play it until their admirable 1958 production, and Marlowe's quatercentenary in 1964 saw its most notable performance at Leicester (in a production too briefly transferred to the Arts Theatre, London). It has also, as one might expect, received two very satisfactory productions on radio, the last as recently as March 1967; sound broadcasting admirably suits its exploratory intellectual and emotional quality.

THE PLAY

Whether *Edward the Second* was written before or after *Doctor Faustus*, few critics fail to place it among the most mature of Marlowe's works, though Maxwell has already been quoted on its essentially derivative quality and Muriel Bradbrook (in *Themes and Conventions of Elizabethan Tragedy*, 1935) dissents still more comprehensively:

> *Edward II* is generally acclaimed as Marlowe's greatest dramatic success; but this is only possible by ignoring Elizabethan standards, and judging purely on 'construction'. As poetic drama, the last speech of Edward is inferior to the last speech of Faustus or even to the early soliloquies of *The Jew of Malta*, and how it is possible to fail as poetry and succeed as drama is not easy to understand . . . In *Edward II* there is no central feeling or theme; it is merely a history.

F. P. Wilson tacitly comments on this last phrase of Professor Bradbrook's (in *Marlowe and the Early Shakespeare*, 1953):

> Anyone who doubts whether Marlowe's gifts were really dramatic would do well to read Holinshed's account of the reign of Edward II and see with what art of selection, condensation, and adaptation Marlowe has shaped out of the chronicle history of a disagreeable reign an historical tragedy . . . Historical dating and historical sequence he regarded as wholly within his control if it led to economy and coherence, above all if it led to the balance of dramatic power.

It may however be necessary to question Marlowe's central concern with history and external event, here or in *The Massacre at Paris*, and indeed F. P. Wilson implies as much in his concluding judgment on this play: 'Marlowe never returned to the theme of English history, as Shakespeare did again and again. He went on to write *Doctor Faustus* and there he fulfilled himself.' Yet even this qualification belies the profound exploration of motive and causation of providence and the ironies of kingship, with which all writers in the fifteen-nineties were preoccupied, whether in Drayton's moralised 'epics', Daniel's *Civil Wars*, the cycles of Shakespeare, or Marlowe's progressive intensity from *Tamburlaine* through *The Massacre at Paris* to *Edward the Second*. For the problems may be stated several ways according to the several preoccupations of the writers. For some, concerned with the ethics of rebellion (and here the 'Barons' wars' trespass on Jack Cade's territory), the conflict may be crudely summarised as a tension between damnable regicide and justifiable tyrannicide. More universally, all the writers are preoccupied with the ironic disparity between status and person; and here the fall of

Edward by infatuation, the emergence of Edward III to royal dignity, the rise of Henry V in power to match his office, the mystical intensity of Cranmer's baptismal oration in the last scene of *Henry the Eighth*, all these are mutations of the single theme, the ambiguities and glories of the regal office.

Pervading these themes, a further metaphysical problem was still more central to the writers' intentions and concerns. Again it may be tersely summarised as the intellectual tension between immutable providence and the vagaries of chance; or, in human terms, between man's destiny predetermined by an omniscient, omnipotent deity and his own part in shaping that destiny (by his grace, *virtù*, or sin) within or in defiance of the divine will. The possibilities of theological variation within these definitions were explored more vigorously in the sixteenth century than at any other period of christendom; as a motive-power for dramatic character or the varied shaping of plot no metaphysical problem has been so formative.

The nature of these speculations as they emerge in Elizabethan drama is admirably stated in the variant long titles of *Edward the Second*. The 1594 and 1598 title-pages between them isolate three tragic motives: 'the troublesome raigne and lamentable death of Edward'; 'the tragicall fall of proud Mortymer'; and 'the life and death of Peirs Gaueston, the great Earle of Cornewall, and mighty fauorite of king Edward'. All three involve the tragic fall of men in high estate but all three are different in their implication both in individual moral responsibility and in the assumption of a moral universe (or its absence).

The king is not unaware of the claims of majesty; there are moments (sporadic but frequent enough to tell) when he behaves with decisive dignity, a swift and courageous authority and a recollection on more than one occasion of an inherited royalty, matter for pride or pathos according to his circumstance—'when the imperial lion's flesh is gored'; 'when I call to mind I am a king'; 'I bear the name of king'—and this regality is given supernatural sanctions and its denial erected to another plane, 'martyred with endless torments'. Edward's betrayal of this royal status and its obligations is wilful, and recognised as such; for at the baronial demand for Gaveston's banishment, the king's abdication of responsibility is unequivocal:

> . . . sooner shall the sea o'erwhelm my land
> Than bear the ship that shall transport thee hence.

This use of an elemental metaphor, of a cosmic deluge, was no casual choice; it was a potent image long before it became trans-figured in King Lear's invocation of the roaring sea.

'The life and death of Peirs Gaueston', though so intimately involved in Edward's fate, carried many implications different from his. That he was the type of the corrupting courtier may be seen in the reported remark of Robert Parsons in 1592 that Burghley's power at the court was 'far more noysome and pernitious to the realme' than that of Gaveston at Edward's court. We must be clear about the nature of this reprehension of Gaveston; the matter condemned was the intensity, the inordinacy of the affection, not its quality. The police-court overtones of our term 'homosexuality' are quite different from the complexity of a relationship which can cite classical and biblical instances of friendship, while importing the sexual overtones in the words 'wanton', 'lascivious' and 'die'. Ultimately the condemnation of Edward lies in the frivolity with which the very realm itself is set aside for his 'minion':

> Ere my sweet Gaveston shall part from me
> This isle shall fleet upon the ocean
> And wander to the unfrequented Ind.

With Mortimer and his relations with Isabella we move into a wholly different area of reference. The barons make their stand for order and good government against the softer indulgences of Edward's court, and Mortimer, a natural leader in the realm of policy, is at first engaging in his plain-spoken candour. As we shall see, there is more than a little ambiguity in the guilt which Marlowe's contemporaries ascribed to Mortimer and Isabella's love and in the main course of *Edward the Second* this is a relatively subordinate theme. Predominating is the slow corruption of power, its increasing attrition upon the character of Mortimer and upon events, as a neutral, amoral 'policy' thrusts aside the legitimate claims of even a defective king upon the loyalty of his subjects. The Machiavellian *virtù*, the demands of *Realpolitik* oust the traditional homogeneity of a natural law which made known its imperatives throughout the created order, of Nature and of Man. For Richard Hooker 'obedience of creatures [i.e. all creatures, from angels to the inanimate, along the whole scale of being] to the law of nature is the stay of the whole world'. Edward and Gaveston break in their several ways certain aspects of this 'law of nature', Edward by the neglect of duty, both of them by inordinate affection. But Mortimer does not simply break laws; his philosophy sets the old law aside. The king in his final imprisonment and sufferings understands this truth. Even while he expresses a mediaeval *contemptus mundi*, affecting to

> despise this transitory pomp
> [To] sit for aye enthronised in heaven

he realises that voluntarily to relinquish the crown is an assault upon
the reign of law itself:

> Here receive my crown;
> Receive it? no, these innocent hands of mine
> Shall not be guilty of so foul a crime,

and he can later, at the penultimate affront of the washing in puddle
water, appeal to the 'Immortal powers' to condemn

> these daring men,
> That wrongs their liege and sovereign, England's king.

These four characters, then, the King and Gaveston, Mortimer
and Isabella, dispose the rest of the *dramatis personae* within two
contrasted universes of law, one assenting to a providential order of
nature, society and the individual man, and asserting also a corres-
ponding moral order of known retribution for sin and crime; the
other an order in which an amoral 'policy' assents to the tenets of
Machiavelli, in which the natural order is subjected to a new
analysis, in which Bacon, Hariot—and Marlowe—are intellectually
at home. Of course this neat division ignores the delicate and shifting
loyalties which blur such intellectual analyses and it is precisely these
tentative exploratory relationships, with their ambiguous modifica-
tions of schematic values, which drama is so well fitted to depict.
Edward the Second no more requires moral assertions, a clear-cut
ascription of praise and blame, than Shakespeare demands for the
characters of Falstaff, Hal or Cleopatra; it is part of Marlowe's
achievement in this play that he sees the interaction of moral
universes with such clarity and complexity within the play world,
while declining to make overt judgments more proper to a moral
treatise.

We are fortunate that the work of Michael Drayton, an exact
contemporary of Marlowe, provides us with an external means of
testing some of these critical assumptions. For Drayton devoted
five historical poems of considerable length to the substance of
Edward II's reign: *Peirs Gaveston*, written in 1593 within some
months of Marlowe's play; *Mortimeriados*, published in 1596, a long
poem on the career and fall of Mortimer; *The Barons Warres*, a
complete and extended reworking of *Mortimeriados* and published
in 1603; and two of *Englands Heroicall Epistles* (1597, modelled on
Ovid's *Heroides*) which skilfully use the letter form, 'Isabel to
Mortimer' and 'Mortimer to Isabel', to extend his analysis of this
relationship which Marlowe treats so sparingly. Taken in conjunction with Ben Jonson's abortive *Fall of Mortimer* (abandoned
after a page or two) and Heywood's *Edward the Third*, these indicate

a remarkable Elizabethan and Jacobean interest in a turbulent period which Shakespeare chose not to handle. Taken together, Drayton's five works greatly extend our knowledge of the commonplace assumptions within which Marlowe worked, and from which in certain particulars he deviated.

Drayton's central assumption of tragedy lies in the irony implicit in Edward's declaration to his captors in *Mortimeriados*:

> I am your King, though wanting Majestie,

which is considerably extended in the weightier measure of *The Barons Warres*:

> If first my Title stedfastly were planted
> Upon a true indubitate Succession,
> Confirm'd by Nations, as by Nature granted,
> Which lawfully deliver'd me Possession;
> You must thinke Heaven sufficiencie hath wanted,
> And so denie it Power; by your oppression,
> > That into question dare thus boldly bring
> > The awfull Right of an anoynted King.

This is pursued through eight more stanzas, with such phrases as 'hallowed Unction' and 'glitt'ring Crowne', leading to the ironic antithesis

> His Head's a Prisoner in a Gaole of Gold

which culminates in the final tragedy:

> But the Sonne climbes, and thrusts the Father downe,
> And thus the Crowned, goes without a Crowne.

These matters are well handled by Drayton who is also, in *The Barons Warres*, aware of the king's dramatic, even theatric role, as the 'Tragedian' for whom Nature had collaborated with Art,

> To teach Despayre to act a Kingly Part.

Marlowe theorises more sparingly than Drayton and, without moralising the analogy of the actor, in fact turns this commonplace into valid theatrical terms, in a terse manipulation of the concept of the *curia regis*, that abstract power of the king's court and the royal presence. The scene follows the capture of the king and subsequently of Kent by Matrevis and Gurney:

> GURNEY
> > Bind him and so convey him to the court.
> KENT
> > Where is the court but here, here is the king
> > And I will visit him, why stay you me?

MATREVIS
> The court is where Lord Mortimer remains,
> Thither shall your honour go, and so farewell.
>
> *Exeunt* MATREVIS *and* GURNEY *with the* KING

KENT
> Oh miserable is that commonweal where lords
> Keep courts, and kings are locked in prison!

Marlowe is here straying no whit beyond the Elizabethan common-places but the intensity of dramatic irony places it beyond Drayton's range. Similarly Drayton, while raising the relation of Mortimer and Isabella to an echo of courtly love and shifting the central interest of the tragedy from the conflict of power where Marlowe strictly retains it, further blunts and makes explicit the relation of Gaveston and Edward. *Peirs Gaueston* in 1593 had opened the possibility of a real conflict between public duty and the private demands of intense friendship, but Drayton's own notes to certain lines in the *Chronicle Historie* (i.e. the *Heroicall Epistles* of 1597) remove the modifying overtones which Marlowe had retained and made the condemnation explicit. Isabella had complained to Mortimer that Edward had scorned her,

> And in my place, upon his Regall Throne,
> To set that Girle-boy, wanton *Gaueston.*

which Drayton further glosses:

> *Noting the effeminacie and luxurious wantonnesse of* Gaueston, *the Kings Minion; his Behauiour and Attire ever so Woman-like, to please the Eye of his lascivious Master.*

Indeed, throughout the considerable extent of Drayton's treatment of this reign there is evidence of a halting between two opinions, on the one hand, of reprehension for a weak king with the consequent justification of rebellion and the treachery of the queen; and on the other hand of admiration for Mortimer (whose noble descent is laboured in *Mortimeriados*) and exaltation of his romantic love while covertly condemning both his rebellion and his ruthlessness. Marlowe makes no such ambiguous play across two moral universes. The very division dramatically into the fall of Gaveston and the fall of Mortimer, related in their two distinct ways to the personal tragedies of Edward and his queen, a division which has earned critical condemnation, is in fact a means of dramatising a dual exploration; in the first half of the play the latent moral implications of a kingdom neglected while private passion is pursued, in the second the conflicting demands of ruthless power denoting order and the innate majesty of the king's person.

This is no mechanical division; themes and verbal echoes link the two parts but in particular the final tragic humiliation of Edward unites the two halves of passion and of power in a horrible parody of moral retribution. This is a subject which public presentation has not unnaturally blurred and which critical treatment has tended to ignore with few brief exceptions. Yet in this extended and carefully-wrought humiliation and death (which even Drayton boldly calls Edward's 'Passion') lies the ultimate key to a critical understanding of Marlowe's dramatic design. Its elements are clear: a king, self-consciously aware of his kingly status yet capriciously denying it in action; an 'upstart' Gaveston (in Marlowe unworthy by his birth of the honour he gains but in Drayton of some dignity); a baron who violently desires order at the price of his allegiance and at the end (like Henry Bolingbroke) achieving his regicide aims through other suborned men, Matrevis, Gurney and the demonic Lightborn. The stages of Edward's humiliation and death are carefully marked and analysed.

It properly begins with the restrained compassion of the Abbot and monks of Neath Abbey (VI. vi) and with Edward's considered stoicism:

> Whilom I was powerful and full of pomp,
> But what is he whom rule and empiry
> Have not in life or death made miserable?
> Come Spencer, come Baldock, come, sit down by me,
> Make trial now of that philosophy.
> That in our famous nurseries of arts
> Thou suckedst from Plato and from Aristotle.
> Father, this life contemplative is heaven,

a momentary insight many degrees removed from the histrionic undertones of Richard II's 'sad stories of the death of kings'.

The next stage in Edward's progress is the direct contact with one who had simply been 'a gloomy fellow', now 'a Mower' prefiguring death, an emblematic technique not unusual in Marlowe and anticipated in the three anonymous figures who greet Gaveston at the opening of the play. With this *memento mori* Edward proceeds to closer insights, both of his friends and of his own pitiful state ('the griefs of private men are soon allayed but not of kings') and the fifth act opens with a carefully modulated rhetorical argument turning on the generalisation

> But what are kings when regiment is gone
> But perfect shadows in a sunshine day?

To Leicester's protest that time is wasting Edward responds with the plea of the dying Faustus that the sun's movement be halted and time cease:

> Stand still you watches of the element,
> All times and seasons rest you in a stay,
> That Edward may be still fair England's king.

But these conjunctions of time, elements and the sun, linking mutability with regality, soon give way to harsher realities; in the second scene Mortimer recalls Tamburlaine's *hubris* in identical terms, as he briefs his instruments, Matrevis and Gurney:

> As thou intendest to ride by Mortimer,
> Who now makes Fortune's wheel turn as he pleases . . .

and the way is open to the final tragedies. The third scene is set noisomely in a dungeon and the king shaved for execution, in 'channel water' from the drains. Lightborn is added to the executioners and his skills are those of the customary Machiavel, of poisoning, strangling and concealed deaths. But his 'braver way' surpasses the Machiavel and trespasses upon the tortures of the damned, difficult for our consciousness to compass. (It is interesting that this is Bert Brecht's most notable failing in his adaptation, *Leben Eduards des Zweiten*, undertaken in 1923 with Feuchtwanger. The death is evasively laconic: Edward has pleaded for the peace of total darkness and after the briefest exchange with Lightborn, asks him why he has come: 'For this', says Lightborn—and stabs him.) The facts of Lightborn's horrifying 'way' are directly and swiftly recorded by Drayton in *The Barons Warres* (Canto V, 65)

> When 'twixt two Beds they clos'd his wearied Course,
> Basely uncovering his most secret Part,
> And without Humane Pittie, or Remorse,
> With a hot spit they thrust him to the Heart.

One or two commentators, tentatively and with embarrassed surprise, have commented on the congruity of this death with his earlier sin. It should in fact occasion no surprise. If Lightborn is a surrogate for Lucifer, anticipating in the fate of Edward the tortures of the damned, he is in a well-established tradition. That suffering and death should bear an appropriate relation to sins committed is a commonplace of mediaeval thought, theological, literary or aesthetic. Dante's assumptions in the *Inferno* were very immediately translated into visual terms as early as the frescoes by Orcogna in the Strozzi Chapel of Santa Maria Novella in Florence. A century later, in 1453, Giovanni di Paolo, in the altar-piece of the Siena Academy, translates Dante's conceptions into very precise images of appropriate suffering (a tradition which persists over the centuries to the drawings and engravings of Blake, Fuseli and Delacroix). A parallel in the treatment of heretics may be cited earlier in Marlowe's century.

By a decree of the Council of Zurich, 7 March 1526, the Lords, the Burgomaster and Great Council under Zwingli 'earnestly endeavoured to turn the misguided and erring Anabaptists from their errors' but without success. It was therefore decreed that those who irregularly baptised others 'will be seized by our Lords, and according to the decree now set forth, *will be drowned without mercy*'. My italics have stressed the parallel to which the sixteenth century, accustomed to public torture and execution, would assent, with horror and acceptance: for the heretic the fire, for the Anabaptist drowning, for Gloucester's lust of the eyes who 'stumbled when he saw', blinding, and for Edward's sin the devilish spit. We who accept a 'theatre of cruelty' with less metaphysical edge should not be surprised at Marlowe's insight.

Marlowe's controlled and mature dramatic handling of this difficult reign found a supple vehicle in the quite unusual variety of the language. Professor Bradbrook wondered 'how it is possible to fail as poetry and succeed as drama' and indeed if there were a substantial measure of poetic failure, failure as drama might possibly be assumed. But this judgment deserves examination. 'The mighty line' is muted in this play and we may agree that 'as poetic drama the last speech of Edward is inferior to the last speech of Faustus', even if 'inferior' begs a few questions. But the dramatic verse of *Edward the Second* has a range of effects unattempted in the other plays. The counterpointing of language begins early. In the opening speech, Gaveston reads a letter from the king containing his ominous words '*share the kingdom* with thy dearest friend'. This shattering of a kingdom's integrity (the wanton determination also of Lear) is echoed just eighty lines later in a quite different key, as Mortimer declares his readiness to destroy the peace of the realm and break his own allegiance in order to rid the kingdom of Gaveston. But the two disintegrating forces, the lasciviousness of Gaveston and the violent practicality of Mortimer, have their equivalents in the verse movement and structure: in the smooth flaccidity of Gaveston,

> Ah words that make me surfeit with delight;
> What greater bliss can hap to Gaveston
> Than live and be the favourite of a king

and the tough, rhetorical argument of Mortimer:

> Mine uncle here, this Earl, and I myself,
> Were sworn to your father at his death
> That he should ne'er return into the realm;
> And know my lord, ere I will break my oath,

> This sword of mine that should offend your foes,
> Shall sleep within the scabbard at thy need,
> And underneath thy banners march who will,
> For Mortimer will hang his armour up.

The dramatic conflict is stated thus squarely and with no ambiguity within the first hundred lines of the play.

Meanwhile, as we have seen, the formal symbolism of the 'three Poor Men' is introduced and Marlowe is prepared at any point in the play to move from naturalistic verse, scarcely more high-pitched than prose conversation, to a formally measured, end-stopped verse-form with quite different functions. Act I, Scene iv is a long, very complex dramatic movement with the greatest variety of speech and situation; at line 170 the queen is given an extended, classically turned soliloquy which is interrupted by the nobles:

LANCASTER
> Look where the sister of the King of France
> Sits wringing of her hands and beats her breast.

WARWICK
> The king I fear hath ill intreated her.

PEMBROKE
> Hard is the heart that injures such a saint.

The formal artifice of these three speeches moves towards the justification of the final rhetorical phrase, 'that injures such a saint'. In a more prosaic structure the phrase would carry a blatant irony; in this setting the irony is held in abeyance, to emerge at her throwing in her lot—and emotions—with Mortimer, while the overt moral judgment is made acceptable.

An even greater complexity of tone may be detected in the passage following the entry of the Bishop of Coventry at I. i, 174. The king greets him with a ponderous irony, 'Whither goes my lord of Coventry so fast?', which is rebuked in the bishop's reply: 'To celebrate your father's exequies'. Gaveston joins the baiting of the prelate,

> and but for reverence of robes,
> Thou shouldst not plod one foot beyond this place,

where 'reverence' and '*plod* one foot' point ironically the king's opening, 'so fast'. Two dramatic factors now unite in making this passage a climactic moment in the play's structure and tone; Gaveston sheds his decadence and moves with sudden vigour into mock-deference, 'saving your reverence', which anticipates the king's command:

> Throw off his golden mitre, rend his stole,
> And in the channel christen him anew.

a speech whose sacrilege anticipates the parallel humiliation of Edward's own end.

A similar careful concern for dramatic pattern recurs through the whole course of the play. Act III, Scene ii has the early entry (at line 32) of Hugh Spencer ('*an old man, father to the young* SPENCER'); with the gravity of age he greets the king formally:

> Long live my sovereign, the noble Edward,
> In peace triumphant, fortunate in wars.

Fifty lines later the king takes leave of the queen, in words that unconsciously and with tragic ambiguity echo those of old Spencer:

> Choose of our lords to bear you company,
> And go in peace, leave us in wars at home.

It might be said with justice that the prevailing tone of this play substitutes a constantly shifting irony for the rhetorical surge of *Tamburlaine*, the savagery of *The Jew of Malta* and the tragic intensity of *Faustus*—with *Edward the Second* deploying, arguably, the most mature means. The central irony of the play stems from the tragic disparity between kingly power and Edward's inability to employ it effectively, yet nowhere is this more finally seen than in the plight of his son after he has succeeded to the regal power:

> KING
> Sweet mother, if I cannot pardon him,
> Entreat my lord Protector for his life.
> QUEEN
> Son, be content, I dare not speak a word.
> KING
> Nor I, and yet methinks I should command.

It is in moments of unobtrusive skill in this manner that Marlowe demonstrates in this play his mature craft, as much as in the unique tragic horror of the theme for which he finds in turn the proper mode and structure.

We have seen that Heywood shifted the historical interest to Edward's son in *Edward the Third*. Marlowe's maturity in craftsmanship is nowhere shown more fully than in his own shift to cosmic order in the closing scenes after Edward's death (Shakespeare and Milton allowed themselves considerably less dramatic time when the tragic passion was spent); indeed Edward himself anticipates the graver, stiller tone in his own dying request to Lightborn:

> Yet stay awhile, forbear thy bloody hand
> And let me see the stroke before it comes
> That even then when I shall lose my life
> My mind may be more steadfast on my God.

This gravity had been prepared for by Edward's tragic ageing; Kent wishes to 'rescue aged Edward from his foes' and in the next scene (V. iii) the king himself reflects that 'thus lives old Edward not relieved by any'. His son moves swiftly to maturity upon achieving authority at his father's death and revenge follows with quick inevitability, with Mortimer revealed as no more in command of fortune's wheel than Tamburlaine in the earlier play.

NOTE ON THE TEXT

THE TEXT for this edition is a modernised version of that of 1594 (reprinted with full bibliographical apparatus by W. W. Greg in the Malone Society Reprint, 1925), collated with the editions of 1598, 1612 and 1622, with the act and scene divisions adopted from the edition of H. B. Charlton and R. D. Waller (1933, revised by F. N. Lees, 1955; the early text had no act and scene divisions, the movement of the play being marked by the principal stage directions).

The first extant edition, though strictly an octavo, has the shape and size of a quarto and is usually referred to as the first quarto. The second quarto was printed in 1598 by Richard Bradock for William Jones; the copy in the Dyce Collection in the Victoria and Albert Museum has been used as the copy for collation with the 1594 version in this present edition. This copy is of peculiar interest in having the first two leaves supplied in manuscript. The argument from its variant readings, with the teasing implication of the date 1593 on the manuscript title-page, should be followed in Greg's discussion in his Malone Society Reprint (pp. vi–viii and x). The 'title-page' and the first page of the text are reproduced from this manuscript on pp. 2 and 3.

Certain of the stage directions and speech prefixes are of importance in determining the nature of the text as we have it. Confusion in assigning speeches between two characters, the Earl of Arundel and Matrevis, leads Greg to the judgment that 'it is hardly possible to avoid the inference (made by Dyce) that the confusion arose owing to the parts of Arundel and Matrevis having been taken by the same actor'. From this, as from some of the textual irregularities recorded above (Malone Society Reprint, pp. xi and xii), it would follow that the piece was printed from a playhouse manuscript, and also apparently that this had undergone some kind of revision for the stage.

The punctuation in this present edition has been made as light as possible to achieve our nearest approximation to the swift and flexible rhetoric of Elizabethan verse and its punctuation. Speech prefixes have been modernised and regularised throughout.

The stage direction, 'SPENCER *reads their names*' at IV. iii, 11 (p. 72) raises a particular problem for production, since the early texts supply no list of those executed. Holinshed, Marlowe's source, supplies their names and a modern production might well follow the same authority:

EDWARD . . .
  Read it Spencer.

SPENCER reads their names

[SPENCER
  'The Lord William Tuchet, the Lord William Fitzwilliam, the Lord Warren de Lisle, the Lord Henry Bradborne, and the Lord William Chenie, barons, with John Page, an esquire, were drawn and hanged at Pomfret.
  And then shortly after, Roger Lord Clifford, John Lord Mowbray, and Sir Gosein d'Eevill, barons, were drawn and hanged at York.
  At Bristow in like manner were executed Sir Henry de Willington and Sir Henry Montford, baronets.
  And at Gloucester, the Lord John Gifford and Sir William Elmebridge, knight.
  And at London, the Lord Henry Teies, baron.
  At Winchelsea, Sir Thomas Culpepper, knight.
  At Windsor, the Lord Francis de Aldham, baron.
  And at Canterbury, the Lord Bartholomew de Badelismere and the Lord Bartholomew de Ashbornham, barons.
  Also at Cardiff, in Wales,Sir William Fleming, knight was executed.
  Divers were executed in their counties, as Sir Thomas Mandit and others.']

EDWARD
  Why so, they barked apace a month ago, . . .

FURTHER READING

Biographical

J. L. Hotson, *The Death of Christopher Marlowe* (London and Harvard, 1925)

C. F. Tucker Brooke, *Life of Marlowe* (with *Dido*), vol. I of the complete Marlowe, ed. R. H. Case (London, 1930–33)

F. S. Boas, *Christopher Marlowe: A Biographical and Critical Study* (Oxford, 1940)

John Bakeless, *The Tragical History of Christopher Marlowe*, 2 vols. (Cambridge, Mass., 1942)

Critical Studies

U. M. Ellis-Fermor, *Christopher Marlowe* (London, 1927)

P. H. Kocher, *Christopher Marlowe* (Chapel Hill, 1946)

M. M. Mahood, *Poetry and Humanism* (London, 1950)

F. P. Wilson, *Marlowe and the Early Shakespeare* (Oxford, 1953)

Harry Levin, *Christopher Marlowe: The Overreacher* (London, 1954)

J. B. Steane, *Marlowe* (Cambridge, 1964)

Brian Morris (ed.), *Christopher Marlowe* (Mermaid
Critical Commentaries; London, 1968)

Clifford Leech has assembled an excellent anthology of essays on Marlowe in the Prentice-Hall series, Twentieth Century Views, 1964 and his own essay, 'Marlowe's *Edward II*: Power and Suffering', *Critical Quarterly*, vol. I, number 3, 1959, is the best critical essay on the play.

For the place of *Edward the Second* in the development of the History Play see:

E. M. W. Tillyard, *Shakespeare's History Plays* (London, 1944)

L. B. Campbell, *Shakespeare's Histories* (San Marino, Calif., 1947)

Wolfgang Clemen, *English Tragedy before Shakespeare* (1955; English translation, London, 1961)

Irving Ribner, *The English History Play in the Age of Shakespeare* (Princeton, 1957)

Critical Aids:

C. Crawford, *Marlowe Concordance*, 5 vols. (Louvain, 1911–32)

S. A. Tannenbaum, *Marlowe: A Concise Bibliography* (New York, 1937; supplement 1947)

THE ILLUSTRATIONS

On the next three pages are reproduced:

p. 1, The title-page (A1 Recto) of the 1598 quarto.

pp. 2 and 3, the 'title-page' and the first page of the manuscript-inset in the 1598 copy from the Dyce Collection in the Victoria and Albert Museum, replacing the pages missing in that copy (see p. xxvii, Note on the Text).

The troublesome

raigne and lamentable death
of Edward the second, King of
England: with the tragicall
fall of proud *Mortimer:*

And also the life and death of *Peirs Gaueston,*
the great Earle of Cornewall, *and mighty*
fauorite of king *Edward* the second, as it was
publiquely acted by the right honorable
the Earle of Pembrooke his
seruantes.

Written by Chri. Marlow *Gent.*

Imprinted at London by Richard Bradocke,
for William Iones dwelling neere Holbourne conduit,
at the signe of the Gunne. 1 5 9 8.

THE

troublesome Raigne and
lamentable death of Edward
the second King of England
with the tragicall fall of proude
Mortimer

As it was sondry times publiquely
acted in the honorable Cittie of
London. By the right honorable
the Earle of Pembroke his
Seruants

Written by Chri: Mar: Gent

Imprinted at London for William Iones
dwelling neere Holborne Conduit at
the Signe of y Gunne. 1593.

The troublesome Raigne & lamentable
death of Edward the second King of
England: with the tragicall fall of
proude Mortimer.

Enter Gaueston reading of a letter that was
brought him from the King.

Gauest. My father is deceast, come Gaueston,
and share the Kingdome with thy dearest freind:
Ah wordes that make me surfet with delight!
What greater blisse can hap to Gaueston,
Then liue & be the fauourite of a King?
Sweete Prince I come; these thy amorous lines,
might haue enforc't me to haue swum from France,
and like Leander gasp'd vpon the sand,
So thou wouldst smile, & take me in thine armes
The sight of London to my exild eyes,
is as Elizium to a new come soule,
Not that I loue the Cittie or the men,
But that it harbors him I hould soe deare,
The King, vpon whose bosome let me die
and with the world be still at enmitie.
What neede the arctick people loue starre light
to whom the Sun shines both by day & night?
Farewell base stooping to ye Lordly Peeres
my knee shall bowe to none but to the King
Its for the multitude, that are but sparkes
bak't vp in embers of their pouertie —
tantum: Ile fawne first on the wind
that glanceth at my lips & flieth away,
But how now what are these?

            Enter 3. poore men
Poore men. Such as desire yor worships seruice.
Gauest. What canst thou doe?
1. poor. I can ride.
Gau: But I haue no horses; what art thou
2. poor. A traueller.
Gauest. Let me see, thou wouldst do well
to waitt at my trencher, & tell me lies at dinner
& as I like your discoursing Ile haue you.
And what art thou?

[Dramatis Personae

KING EDWARD THE SECOND
PRINCE EDWARD *his son, afterwards* King Edward the Third
EDMUND EARL OF KENT, *brother of* King Edward the Second
PIERCE DE GAVESTON, Earl of Cornwall
GUY EARL OF WARWICK
THOMAS EARL OF LANCASTER
AYMER DE VALENCE, Earl of Pembroke
EDMUND FITZALAN, Earl of Arundel
HENRY EARL OF LEICESTER, *brother of the* Earl of Lancaster
SIR THOMAS BERKELEY
ROGER MORTIMER OF CHIRK (Mortimer Senior)
ROGER MORTIMER OF WIGMORE (Mortimer Junior) *his nephew*
HUGH LE DESPENSER (Spencer Senior)
HUGH LE DESPENSER (Spencer Junior) *his son*
ROBERT WINCHELSEY, Archbishop ('Bishop') of Canterbury
WALTER LANGTON, Bishop of Coventry
JOHN STRATFORD, Bishop of Winchester
ROBERT BALDOCK
HENRY DE BEAUMONT
SIR WILLIAM TRUSSEL
THOMAS GURNEY
SIR JOHN MALTRAVERS ('Matrevis')
LIGHTBORN
SIR JOHN OF HAINAULT
LEVUNE
RICE AP HOWELL
THE ABBOT OF NEATH

QUEEN ISABELLA, *daughter of the* King of France
LADY MARGARET DE CLARE, *the* King's niece, *daughter of the* Earl of
    Gloucester *and wife* of Gaveston

THREE POOR MEN	THE HERALD
THE MOWER	THE CHAMPION

Lords, Ladies, Attendants, Messengers, Soldiers, Monks]

Dramatis Personae
    There is no list of characters in the early editions. There are some curious
    features in the speech-prefixes of the texts on which the present edition
    is based: BERKELEY is spelt Bartley; SPENCER is spelt Spenser; the

ARCHBISHOP OF CANTERBURY is called simply *Bishop of Canterbury* (a very curious error for Marlowe to commit especially since Holinshed, his source, has 'the Archbishop of Canterburie'); there is a tendency to confuse ARUNDEL, one of the Barons, with MATREVIS who appears late in the play: Dyce and Greg assume this to be an indication that the parts were doubled by the same actor.

One or two of the characters are invented by Marlowe, notably LIGHTBORN (see Introduction, p. xiii) and LEVUNE. The historical relations between the characters are as faithfully preserved as one would expect, within the necessary compression of the time-sequence to constitute a swift-moving tragedy; one notable manipulation of fact is the appearance of the Earl of Kent in the early scenes of the play. He was half-brother to Edward II and seventeen years his junior, though the disparity in age is concealed in the action of the play.

EDWARD THE SECOND

[Act I, Scene i]

Enter GAVESTON *reading on a letter that was brought him from*
the KING

GAVESTON
 'My father is deceased; come Gaveston,
 And share the kingdom with thy dearest friend.'
 Ah words that make me surfeit with delight;
 What greater bliss can hap to Gaveston
 Than live and be the favourite of a king?   5
 Sweet prince I come; these, these thy amorous lines
 Might have enforced me to have swum from France.
 And like Leander gasped upon the sand,
 So thou wouldst smile and take me in thy arms.
 The sight of London to my exiled eyes   10
 Is as Elysium to a new-come soul;
 Not that I love the city or the men
 But that it harbours him I hold so dear,
 The king, upon whose bosom let me die
 And with the world be still at enmity.   15
 What need the arctic people love starlight,
 To whom the sun shines both by day and night?
 Farewell base stooping to the lordly peers;
 My knee shall bow to none but to the king.
 As for the multitude that are but sparks,   20
 Raked up in embers of their poverty,
 Tanti; I'll fan first on the wind,

22 *Tanti* so much for that

---

3 *surfeit.* It is characteristic of the temper of the opening scenes that the
 sense of appetite should be appealed to. Compare Shakespeare's ambiguous relation of love and appetite throughout *Troilus and Cressida* and
 particularly the curious relation in the opening speech of *Twelfth Night*:
 'music . . . the food of love . . . surfeiting, the appetite may sicken and
 so die'.
8 *Leander,* cf. Marlowe's narrative poem *Hero and Leander.*
16–21 *starlight, sun, sparks, embers,* an extended play on the relation between
 the sun as the principal light of the heavens and kingship and degree
 among men.

That glanceth at my lips and flieth away.
But how now, what are these?

Enter three POOR MEN

POOR MEN
Such as desire your worship's service. 25
GAVESTON
What canst thou do?
FIRST MAN
I can ride.
GAVESTON
But I have no horses. What art thou?
SECOND MAN
A traveller.
GAVESTON
Let me see, thou wouldst do well to wait at my trencher and 30
tell me lies at dinner time, and as I like your discoursing, I'll
have you. And what art thou?
THIRD MAN
A soldier that hath served against the Scot.
GAVESTON
Why, there are hospitals for such as you,
I have no war and therefore, sir be gone. 35
THIRD MAN
Farewell, and perish by a soldier's hand
That wouldst reward them with an hospital.
GAVESTON
[*Aside*] Ay, ay, these words of his move me as much
As if a goose should play the porpintine
And dart her plumes, thinking to pierce my breast. 40
But yet it is no pain to speak men fair;
I'll flatter these, and make them live in hope.—
You know that I came lately out of France
And yet I have not viewed my lord the king;
If I speed well I'll entertain you all. 45
ALL
We thank your worship.

30 *trencher* plate; hence place at table
39 *porpintine* porcupine

---

24 s.d. *Enter three Poor Men.* Marlowe not infrequently employs characters
(like the Mower late in the play) who are both living men and dramatic,
functional symbols; compare the exactly similar use of the Gardener in
Shakespeare's early play, *Richard the Second.*

GAVESTON
  I have some business; leave me to myself.
ALL
  We will wait here about the court.   *Exeunt*
GAVESTON
  Do. These are not men for me;
  I must have wanton poets, pleasant wits,   50
  Musicians, that with touching of a string
  May draw the pliant king which way I please;
  Music and poetry is his delight,
  Therefore I'll have Italian masques by night,
  Sweet speeches, comedies and pleasing shows,   55
  And in the day when he shall walk abroad,
  Like sylvan nymphs my pages shall be clad,
  My men like satyrs grazing on the lawns
  Shall with their goat feet dance an antic hay;
  Sometime a lovely boy in Dian's shape,   60
  With hair that gilds the water as it glides,
  Crownets of pearl about his naked arms,
  And in his sportful hands an olive-tree
  To hide those parts which men delight to see,
  Shall bathe him in a spring, and there hard by   65
  One like Actaeon peeping through the grove
  Shall by the angry goddess be transformed,
  And running in the likeness of an hart,
  By yelping hounds pulled down and seem to die;
  Such things as these best please his majesty.   70
  My lord! Here comes the king and the nobles
  From the parliament; I'll stand aside.

Enter the KING, LANCASTER, MORTIMER SENIOR, MORTIMER
JUNIOR, EDMUND EARL OF KENT, GUY EARL OF WARWICK, *etc.*

EDWARD
  Lancaster.
LANCASTER
  My lord.

---

50 *wanton poets.* Gaveston's references to the arts and entertainments are
    ambiguous, both appreciative of them (as against the rougher, 'philis-
    tine' barons) and cynically employing them to seduce Edward, 'the
    pliant king', from his regal duties.
60–69 *Dian . . . Actaeon.* Marlowe, like Shakespeare, makes frequent use
    of Ovid's *Metamorphoses*, in the third book of which Actaeon is changed
    to a hart for having seen Diana bathing.

GAVESTON
    [*Aside*] That Earl of Lancaster do I abhor.   75
EDWARD
    Will you not grant me this? [*Aside*] in spite of them
    I'll have my will and these two Mortimers
    That cross me thus shall know I am displeased.
MORTIMER SENIOR
    If you love us, my lord, hate Gaveston.
GAVESTON
    [*Aside*] That villain Mortimer! I'll be his death.   80
MORTIMER JUNIOR
    Mine uncle here, this Earl, and I myself,
    Were sworn to your father at his death
    That he should ne'er return into the realm;
    And know my lord, ere I will break my oath,
    This sword of mine that should offend your foes,   85
    Shall sleep within the scabbard at thy need,
    And underneath thy banners march who will,
    For Mortimer will hang his armour up.
GAVESTON
    [*Aside*] *Mort Dieu!*
EDWARD
    Well Mortimer, I'll make thee rue these words;   90
    Beseems it thee to contradict thy king?
    Frownest thou thereat aspiring Lancaster?
    The sword shall plane the furrows of thy brows
    And hew these knees that now are grown so stiff;
    I will have Gaveston, and you shall know   95
    What danger 'tis to stand against your king.
GAVESTON
    [*Aside*] Well done, Ned!
LANCASTER
    My lord, why do you thus incense your peers,
    That naturally would love and honour you?
    But for that base and obscure Gaveston,   100

84 ff. Mortimer's flagrant breach of allegiance answers to the social discord
    which would be noted by an Elizabethan audience in the opening lines
    of the play: 'Come Gaveston, And *share the kingdom*'. Shakespeare
    appeals to the same horror of social and political discord inherent in the
    division of a kingdom in the first scenes of *King Lear*.
89 *Mort Dieu*, a reference to the dubious etymology of the name Mortimer,
    made explicit below, II. iii, 22–3, 'that dead sea, Whereof we got the
    name of Mortimer'. Gaveston has already begun the pun (I. i, 80):
    'That villain Mortimer! I'll be his death'.

Four earldoms have I besides Lancaster,
Derby, Salisbury, Lincoln, Leicester,
These will I sell to give my soldiers pay,
Ere Gaveston shall stay within the realm;
Therefore if he be come, expel him straight.   105

KENT
Barons and earls, your pride hath made me mute,
But now I'll speak, and to the proof I hope:
I do remember in my father's days,
Lord Percy of the North being highly moved
Braved Mowbery in presence of the king,   110
For which, had not his highness loved him well,
He should have lost his head, but with his look
The undaunted spirit of Percy was appeased,
And Mowbery and he were reconciled;
Yet dare you brave the king unto his face;   115
Brother revenge it, and let these their heads
Preach upon poles for trespass of their tongues.

WARWICK
O, our heads!

EDWARD
Ay yours, and therefore I would wish you grant . . .

WARWICK
Bridle thy anger gentle Mortimer.   120

MORTIMER JUNIOR
I cannot, nor I will not; I must speak;
Cousin, our hands I hope shall fence our heads
And strike off his that makes you threaten us.
Come uncle, let us leave the brainsick king
And henceforth parley with our naked swords.   125

MORTIMER SENIOR
Wiltshire hath men enough to save our heads.

WARWICK
All Warwickshire will love him for my sake.

LANCASTER
And northward Gaveston hath many friends.
Adieu my lord, and either change your mind
Or look to see the throne where you should sit   130

110 *Braved* outfaced

117–125 *Preach . . . tongues . . . parley*. The pattern of metaphors through-
    out the play is more elaborately complex than is usually recognised (see
    Introduction p. xxii ff). 'Words' are frequently active instruments in
    Marlowe, as in Tamburlaine's 'working words'.

To float in blood and at thy wanton head
The glozing head of thy base minion thrown.

Exeunt nobles [except KENT]

EDWARD

I cannot brook these haughty menaces;
Am I a king and must be overruled?
Brother, display my ensigns in the field;   135
I'll bandy with the barons and the earls,
And either die, or live with Gaveston.

GAVESTON

I can no longer keep me from my lord.

EDWARD

What Gaveston! welcome! kiss not my hand;
Embrace me Gaveston as I do thee;   140
Why shouldst thou kneel; knowest thou not who I am?
Thy friend, thy self, another Gaveston;
Not Hylas was more mourned of Hercules
Than thou hast been of me since thy exile.

GAVESTON

And since I went from hence, no soul in hell   145
Hath felt more torment than poor Gaveston.

EDWARD

I know it. [*To* KENT] Brother, welcome home my friend.
[*To* GAVESTON] Now let the treacherous Mortimers conspire,
And that high-minded Earl of Lancaster;
I have my wish, in that I joy thy sight,   150
And sooner shall the sea o'erwhelm my land
Than bear the ship that shall transport thee hence.
I here create thee Lord High Chamberlain,
Chief Secretary to the State and me,
Earl of Cornwall, King and Lord of Man.   155

GAVESTON

My lord, these titles far exceed my worth.

132 *glozing* flattering *minion* favourite

---

143 *Hylas . . . Hercules*, one of Marlowe's frequent classical references to
    male friendship, by no means always bearing modern connotations of
    homosexuality. Hercules had killed the father of Hylas but, having taken
    the boy with him among the Argonauts, lost him to the Naiads at Mysia.
151 *sea o'erwhelm my land*. The most powerful natural catastrophe, a cosmic
    disaster repeating the Deluge, seen at its most dramatically significant
    in the third act of *King Lear*. Here it initiates an increasing levity in
    Edward's character through lines 156–169 to the final descent to the
    word *fancy*. Gaveston's following speech points the levity of the king in
    its reference to 'Caesar . . . triumphant'.

KENT
   Brother, the least of these may well suffice
   For one of greater birth than Gaveston.
EDWARD
   Cease brother, for I cannot brook these words;
   [*To* GAVESTON] Thy worth, sweet friend, is far above my gifts,   160
   Therefore to equal it receive my heart;
   If for these dignities thou be envied,
   I'll give thee more, for but to honour thee
   Is Edward pleased with kingly regiment.
   Fearest thou thy person? thou shalt have a guard;   165
   Want'st thou gold? go to my treasury;
   Wouldst thou be loved and feared? receive my seal;
   Save or condemn, and in our name command;
   Whatso thy mind affects or fancy likes.
GAVESTON
   It shall suffice me to enjoy your love,   170
   Which whiles I have I think myself as great
   As Caesar riding in the roman street,
   With captive kings at his triumphant car.

                Enter the BISHOP OF COVENTRY

EDWARD
   Whither goes my lord of Coventry so fast?
BISHOP
   To celebrate your father's exequies;   175
   But is that wicked Gaveston returned?
EDWARD
   Ay priest, and lives to be revenged on thee
   That wert the only cause of his exile.
GAVESTON
   'Tis true, and but for reverence of these robes,
   Thou shouldst not plod one foot beyond this place.   180
BISHOP
   I did no more than I was bound to do,
   And Gaveston unless thou be reclaimed,

164 *regiment* rule
169 *affects* likes, desires

176–187 A further passage of complex images traversing the words 'wicked
   . . . reverence . . . mitre . . . stole'. In the contrast between the disintegrating quality of Gaveston and the reverent status of the bishop
   there is a growing irony until line 187, 'And in the channel christen him
   anew', with its macabre prefiguring of Edward's final humiliation and
   death.

As then I did incense the parliament,
So will I now, and thou shalt back to France.

GAVESTON

Saving your reverence, you must pardon me.   185

EDWARD

Throw off his golden mitre, rend his stole,
And in the channel christen him anew.

KENT

Ah brother, lay not violent hands on him,
For he'll complain unto the see of Rome.

GAVESTON

Let him complain unto the see of hell,   190
I'll be revenged on him for my exile.

EDWARD

No, spare his life but seize upon his goods.
Be thou lord bishop, and receive his rents,
And make him serve thee as thy chaplain,
I give him thee; here use him as thou wilt.   195

GAVESTON

He shall to prison and there die in bolts.

EDWARD

Ay, to the Tower, the Fleet, or where thou wilt.

BISHOP

For this offence be thou accurst of God.

EDWARD

Who's there? convey this priest to the Tower.

BISHOP

True, true.   200

EDWARD

But in the meantime Gaveston, away,
And take possession of his house and goods,
Come follow me, and thou shalt have my guard
To see it done and bring thee safe again.

GAVESTON

What should a priest do with so fair a house?   205
A prison may beseem his holiness.   [*Exeunt*]

187 *channel* drain, gutter

193–194 In legal terms Gaveston is made an escheator, receiving the
revenues of the see. The grave significance of this action is emphasised
in the next scene, I. ii, 45, 'the bishopric of Coventry is his'.

199 This extends the ironic play on the goods and revenues of the bishopric.
The Fleet (l. 197) was a debtors' prison, while 'convey' is a legal term
of financial conversion (conveyance); vulgarly it also implied theft.

[Act I, Scene ii]

Enter both the MORTIMERS, WARWICK *and* LANCASTER

WARWICK
'Tis true, the Bishop is in the Tower,
And goods and body given to Gaveston.
LANCASTER
What! will they tyrannise upon the Church?
Ah, wicked king! accursed Gaveston!
This ground which is corrupted with their steps,   5
Shall be their timeless sepulchre or mine.
MORTIMER JUNIOR
Well, let that peevish Frenchman guard him sure;
Unless his breast be sword-proof he shall die.
MORTIMER SENIOR
How now, why droops the Earl of Lancaster?
MORTIMER JUNIOR
Wherefore is Guy of Warwick discontent?   10
LANCASTER
That villain Gaveston is made an earl.
MORTIMER SENIOR
An earl!
WARWICK
Ay, and besides, Lord Chamberlain of the Realm,
And Secretary too, and Lord of Man.
MORTIMER SENIOR
We may not nor we will not suffer this.   15
MORTIMER JUNIOR
Why post we not from hence to levy men?
LANCASTER
'My lord of Cornwall' now at every word,
And happy is the man whom he vouchsafes
For vailing of his bonnet one good look.
Thus arm in arm, the king and he doth march;   20
Nay more, the guard upon his lordship waits,
And all the court begins to flatter him.
WARWICK
Thus leaning on the shoulder of the king,
He nods, and scorns, and smiles at those that pass.

19 *vailing* doffing

6 *timeless*, a pun on 'untimely' and 'eternal'.

MORTIMER SENIOR
  Doth no man take exceptions at the slave?   25
LANCASTER
  All stomach him, but none dare speak a word.
MORTIMER JUNIOR
  Ah that bewrays their baseness, Lancaster;
  Were all the earls and barons of my mind,
  We'll hale him from the bosom of the king,
  And at the court-gate hang the peasant up,   30
  Who, swollen with venom of ambitious pride,
  Will be the ruin of the realm and us.

Enter the BISHOP OF CANTERBURY [*with a chaplain*]

WARWICK
  Here comes my lord of Canterbury's grace.
LANCASTER
  His countenance bewrays he is displeased.
BISHOP
  First were his sacred garments rent and torn,   35
  Then laid they violent hands upon him next,
  Himself imprisoned, and his goods asseized,
  This certify the Pope; away, take horse.
LANCASTER
  My lord, will you take arms against the king?
BISHOP
  What need I? God himself is up in arms   40
  When violence is offered to the Church.
MORTIMER JUNIOR
  Then will you join with us that be his peers
  To banish or behead that Gaveston?
BISHOP
  What else my lords? for it concerns me near;
  The bishopric of Coventry is his.   45

Enter the QUEEN

MORTIMER JUNIOR
  Madam, whither walks your majesty so fast?

26 *stomach* resent
27 *bewrays* betrays
37 *asseized* seized upon

32 s.d. *Bishop of Canterbury*. See above, p. 6, on *Dramatis Personae*. The
  use of 'Bishop' for 'Archbishop' is the more surprising by contrast with
  the formality of l. 33, 'my lord of Canterbury's *grace*'.

QUEEN

    Unto the forest, gentle Mortimer,
    To live in grief and baleful discontent,
    For now my lord the king regards me not,
    But dotes upon the love of Gaveston;   50
    He claps his cheeks and hangs about his neck,
    Smiles in his face and whispers in his ears,
    And when I come, he frowns, as who should say,
    'Go whither thou wilt seeing I have Gaveston.'

MORTIMER SENIOR

    Is it not strange that he is thus bewitched?   55

MORTIMER JUNIOR

    Madam, return unto the court again;
    That sly inveigling Frenchman we'll exile,
    Or lose our lives; and yet ere that day come
    The king shall lose his crown, for we have power,
    And courage too, to be revenged at full.   60

BISHOP

    But yet lift not your swords against the king.

LANCASTER

    No, but we'll lift Gaveston from hence.

WARWICK

    And war must be the means, or he'll stay still.

QUEEN

    Then let him stay, for rather than my lord
    Shall be oppressed by civil mutinies,   65
    I will endure a melancholy life,
    And let him frolic with his minion.

BISHOP

    My lords, to ease all this but hear me speak;
    We and the rest that are his counsellors
    Will meet and with a general consent   70
    Confirm his banishment with our hands and seals.

LANCASTER

    What we confirm the king will frustrate.

MORTIMER JUNIOR

    Then may we lawfully revolt from him.

---

47 *Unto the forest.* Elizabethan drama is ambivalent on the significance
    of the forest or waste land. It might signify a rural retreat, a place
    of renewal; conversely it represented alien forces, the antithesis of
    civilisation, as in *Macbeth, King Lear* or *The Winter's Tale.* Much of
    As You Like It is a formal debate on these contrasted significances.
61–62 *lift . . . swords; lift Gaveston.* The ironic pun underlines the pre-
    vailing theme of rebellion.

WARWICK
But say, my lord, where shall this meeting be?
BISHOP
At the New Temple.   75
MORTIMER JUNIOR
Content.
BISHOP
And in the mean-time I'll intreat you all,
To cross to Lambeth and there stay with me.
LANCASTER
Come then, let's away.
MORTIMER JUNIOR
Madam, farewell.   70
QUEEN
Farewell, sweet Mortimer, and for my sake,
Forbear to levy arms against the king.
MORTIMER JUNIOR
Ay, if words will serve; if not, I must.   [*Exeunt*]

[Act I, Scene iii]

Enter GAVESTON *and the* EARL OF KENT

GAVESTON
Edmund the mighty prince of Lancaster,
That hath more earldoms than an ass can bear,
And both the Mortimers, two goodly men,
With Guy of Warwick, that redoubted knight,
Are gone towards Lambeth; there let them remain. *Exeunt*   5

[Act I, Scene iv]

Enter NOBLES [*and* BISHOP OF CANTERBURY]

LANCASTER
Here is the form of Gaveston's exile;
May it please your lordship to subscribe your name.

1–5 This complete scene in five lines is a swift theatrical stroke, eminently
    successful in Marlowe's theatre. Its impression of a decisive, ruthless
    Gaveston is given ironic emphasis by being spoken to the Earl of Kent,
    throughout portrayed as a man of integrity. This irony is picked up in
    the words of Mortimer Senior in the next scene concerning Gaveston
    and 'the Earl of Kent who favours him' (l. 34).

BISHOP
Give me the paper.
LANCASTER
Quick, quick, my lord, I long to write my name.
WARWICK
But I long more to see him banished hence.   5
MORTIMER JUNIOR
The name of Mortimer shall fright the king,
Unless he be declined from that base peasant.

Enter the KING *and* GAVESTON

EDWARD
What? are you moved that Gaveston sits here?
It is our pleasure; we will have it so.
LANCASTER
Your grace doth well to place him by your side,   10
For nowhere else the new earl is so safe.
MORTIMER SENIOR
What man of noble birth can brook this sight?
Quam male conveniunt:
See what a scornful look the peasant casts.
PEMBROKE
Can kingly lions fawn on creeping ants?   15
WARWICK
Ignoble vassal that like Phaeton
Aspirest unto the guidance of the sun.

8 *are you moved that Gaveston sits here?* The 'sunk or implied stage direction' is a frequent device of Elizabethan dramatic verse. Here, the word
'sits' carried powerful implications in relation to the Chair Royal, the
throne which dominated the stage. It is taken up, by silent inference,
if the audience completed the quotation hinted at in line 13; Lancaster
has carried on the action of Gaveston's assumption of a royal place ('to
place him by your side', in the second Chair Royal, normally reserved
for the queen) to which Mortimer Senior responds with a garbled reference to Ovid, *Metamorphoses* II, 846, 'Non bene conveniunt, nec *in una
sede* (my italics) morantur, Maiestas et amor'. Golding's translation
skilfully conveys the implication
> Betweene the state of Majestie and love is set such oddes,
> As that they cannot dwell in one.

16 *Phaeton,* the overweening son of Helios, the Sun, who failed to control
his father's chariot, was struck by Jove's thunderbolt and plunged to his
death. The association of arrogance against the kingly image of the Sun
has manifest relevance here.

MORTIMER JUNIOR
  Their downfall is at hand, their forces down;
  We will not thus be faced and overpeered.
EDWARD
  Lay hands on that traitor Mortimer.   20
MORTIMER SENIOR
  Lay hands on that traitor Gaveston.
KENT
  Is this the duty that you owe your king?
WARWICK
  We know our duties; let him know his peers.
EDWARD
  Whither will you bear him? stay or ye shall die.
MORTIMER SENIOR
  We are no traitors, therefore threaten not.   25
GAVESTON
  No, threaten not my lord, but pay them home.
  Were I a king!
MORTIMER JUNIOR
  Thou villain, wherefore talk'st thou of a king
  That hardly art a gentleman by birth?
EDWARD
  Were he a peasant being my minion,   30
  I'll make the proudest of you stoop to him.
LANCASTER
  My lord, you may not thus disparage us;
  Away I say with hateful Gaveston.
MORTIMER SENIOR
  And with the Earl of Kent that favours him.
               [Exeunt attendants with KENT *and* GAVESTON]
EDWARD
  Nay, then lay violent hands upon your king;   35
  Here Mortimer, sit thou in Edward's throne,
  Warwick and Lancaster, wear you my crown;
  Was ever king thus overruled as I?
LANCASTER
  Learn then to rule us better and the realm.

---

19 *overpeered*. Marlowe has an unusual proliferation of words compounded
  with 'over-'; compare 'overruled' below at l. 38 and 'overdaring' at
  l. 47; and, elsewhere in Marlowe: overbear, overjoys, overlook, overstretched, overthrow, overwatched, overwhelm, overwoo. These divide
  themselves between simple stylistic intensives and a constant sense of
  'overreaching'.

MORTIMER JUNIOR
What we have done, our heart-blood shall maintain.   40
WARWICK
Think you that we can brook this upstart pride?
EDWARD
Anger and wrathful fury stops my speech.
BISHOP
Why are you moved? be patient my lord,
And see what we your counsellors have done.
MORTIMER JUNIOR
My lords, now let us all be resolute,   45
And either have our wills, or lose our lives.
EDWARD
Meet you for this, proud overdaring peers?
Ere my sweet Gaveston shall part from me
This isle shall fleet upon the ocean
And wander to the unfrequented Ind.   50
BISHOP OF CANTERBURY
You know that I am legate to the Pope;
On your allegiance to the see of Rome,
Subscribe as we have done to his exile.
MORTIMER JUNIOR
Curse him if he refuse, and then may we
Depose him and elect another king.   55
EDWARD
Ay there it goes, but yet I will not yield;
Curse me, depose me, do the worst you can.
LANCASTER
Then linger not, my lord, but do it straight.
BISHOP OF CANTERBURY
Remember how the bishop was abused;
Either banish him that was the cause thereof,   60
Or I will presently discharge these lords
Of duty and allegiance due to thee.
EDWARD
    [*Aside*] It boots me not to threat; I must speak fair,—

---

49 *This isle shall fleet.* The shocking levity of the failure to care for the
realm contrasts with the 'simple patriotism' of the barons.

52 *On your allegiance.* This is as disturbing to an Elizabethan audience as
the king's levity noted at l. 49; 'on your allegiance' (frequently used by
Shakespeare's kings) demands instant obedience; used here *to* the king
by the Pope's legate, it has an ominous implication.

54 *Curse,* excommunicate, and therefore release from fealty. The Elizabethan audience had experience also of this papal threat.

The Legate of the Pope will be obeyed:
My lord, you shall be Chancellor of the realm,   65
Thou Lancaster, High Admiral of our fleet,
Young Mortimer and his uncle shall be earls,
And you lord Warwick, President of the North,
And thou [*To* PEMBROKE] of Wales; if this content you not,
Make several kingdoms of this monarchy   70
And share it equally amongst you all,
So I may have some nook or corner left
To frolic with my dearest Gaveston.

BISHOP OF CANTERBURY
Nothing shall alter us, we are resolved.

LANCASTER
Come, come, subscribe.   75

MORTIMER JUNIOR
Why should you love him whom the world hates so?

EDWARD
Because he loves me more than all the world;
Ah, none but rude and savage-minded men
Would seek the ruin of my Gaveston;
You that be noble-born should pity him.   80

WARWICK
You that are princely-born should shake him off;
For shame subscribe and let the lown depart.

MORTIMER SENIOR
Urge him my lord.

BISHOP OF CANTERBURY
Are you content to banish him the realm?

EDWARD
I see I must and therefore am content;   85
Instead of ink I'll write it with my tears.

MORTIMER JUNIOR
The king is love-sick for his minion.

EDWARD
'Tis done, and now accursed hand fall off.

---

82 *lown* rogue, boor (variant of 'loon')

70 *several kingdoms.* The integrity of the realm was Elizabeth's main pre-
   occupation. Deliberately to divide the kingdom and hence to court civil
   war (cf. the opening of *King Lear*) was a king's ultimate dereliction of
   duty.
78–92 *rude . . . savage . . . noble . . . princely . . . common sort,* a carefully
   calculated verbal play on the degrees of society, placing the relationship
   of king, favourite and barons.

LANCASTER
  Give it me, I'll have it published in the streets.
MORTIMER JUNIOR
  I'll see him presently dispatched away.   90
BISHOP OF CANTERBURY
  Now is my heart at ease.
WARWICK   And so is mine.
PEMBROKE
  This will be good news to the common sort.
MORTIMER SENIOR
  Be it or no, he shall not linger here.   *Exeunt* NOBLES
EDWARD
  How fast they run to banish him I love;
  They would not stir, were it to do me good.   95
  Why should a king be subject to a priest?
  Proud Rome, that hatchest such imperial grooms,
  For these thy superstitious taperlights,
  Wherewith thy antichristian churches blaze,
  I'll fire thy crazed buildings and enforce   100
  The papal towers to kiss the lowly ground;
  With slaughtered priests may Tiber's channel swell
  And banks raised higher with their sepulchres;
  As for the peers that back the clergy thus,
  If I be king, not one of them shall live.   105

                   Enter GAVESTON

GAVESTON
  My lord I hear it whispered everywhere,
  That I am banished and must fly the land.
EDWARD
  'Tis true sweet Gaveston; oh, were it false!
  The Legate of the Pope will have it so,
  And thou must hence or I shall be deposed;   110
  But I will reign to be revenged of them,
  And therefore, sweet friend, take it patiently;
  Live where thou wilt, I'll send thee gold enough,
  And long thou shalt not stay, or if thou dost,
  I'll come to thee; my love shall ne'er decline.   115
GAVESTON
  Is all my hope turned to this hell of grief?
EDWARD
  Rend not my heart with thy too piercing words;
  Thou from this land, I from my self am banished.

100 *crazed* shattered

GAVESTON
  To go from hence grieves not poor Gaveston,
  But to forsake you, in whose gracious looks   120
  The blessedness of Gaveston remains,
  For nowhere else seeks he felicity.
EDWARD
  And only this torments my wretched soul,
  That whether I will or no thou must depart;
  Be Governor of Ireland in my stead   125
  And there abide till fortune call thee home.
  Here take my picture and let me wear thine;
  O, might I keep thee here as I do this,
  Happy were I, but now most miserable.
GAVESTON
  'Tis something to be pitied of a king.   130
EDWARD
  Thou shalt not hence; I'll hide thee, Gaveston,
GAVESTON
  I shall be found, and then 'twill grieve me more.
EDWARD
  Kind words and mutual talk makes our grief greater.
  Therefore with dumb embracement let us part;
  Stay Gaveston, I cannot leave thee thus.   135
GAVESTON
  For every look my lord drops down a tear;
  Seeing I must go, do not renew my sorrow.
EDWARD
  The time is little that thou hast to stay
  And therefore give me leave to look my fill,
  But come sweet friend, I'll bear thee on thy way.   140
GAVESTON
  The peers will frown.
EDWARD
  I pass not for their anger; come let's go.
  Oh that we might as well return as go.

                Enter EDMUND *and* QUEEN ISABEL
QUEEN
  Whither goes my lord?
EDWARD
  Fawn not on me, French strumpet; get thee gone.   145
QUEEN
  On whom but on my husband should I fawn?

142 *pass* care

GAVESTON

On Mortimer, with whom, ungentle queen . . .
I say no more; judge you the rest, my lord.

QUEEN

In saying this, thou wrongst me, Gaveston;
Is't not enough, that thou corruptest my lord,   150
And art a bawd to his affections,
But thou must call mine honour thus in question?

GAVESTON

I mean not so; your grace must pardon me.

EDWARD

Thou art too familiar with that Mortimer,
And by thy means is Gaveston exiled,   155
But I would wish thee reconcile the lords,
Or thou shalt ne'er be reconciled to me.

QUEEN

Your highness knows it lies not in my power.

EDWARD

Away then, touch me not; come Gaveston.

QUEEN

Villain, 'tis thou that robbst me of my lord.   160

GAVESTON

Madam, 'tis you that rob me of my lord.

EDWARD

Speak not unto her; let her droop and pine.

QUEEN

Wherein my lord have I deserved these words?
Witness the tears that Isabella sheds,
Witness this heart that sighing for thee breaks,   165
How dear my lord is to poor Isabel.

EDWARD

And witness heaven how dear thou art to me.
There weep, for till my Gaveston be repealed,
Assure thyself thou comst not in my sight.

                    Exeunt EDWARD *and* GAVESTON

QUEEN

Oh miserable and distressed queen!   170
Would when I left sweet France and was embarked,

---

160 ff. These formal, antithetic lines establish, almost by 'ritual' means, the
    severance of relationship between the king and queen. This is confirmed
    by the formal distancing of the tragedy in the queen's soliloquy below
    (ll. 170 ff.) where Circe, Hymen, Juno, Jove and Ganymede establish a
    remote, objective equivalent to her condition.

That charming Circe walking on the waves,
Had changed my shape, or at the marriage day
The cup of Hymen had been full of poison,
Or with those arms that twined about my neck, 175
I had been stifled, and not lived to see
The king my lord thus to abandon me;
Like frantic Juno will I fill the earth
With ghastly murmur of my sighs and cries,
For never doted Jove on Ganymede 180
So much as he on cursed Gaveston;
But that will more exasperate his wrath;
I must entreat him, I must speak him fair,
And be a means to call home Gaveston;
And yet he'll ever dote on Gaveston, 185
And so am I for ever miserable.

Enter the NOBLES *to the* QUEEN

LANCASTER
Look where the sister of the King of France
Sits wringing of her hands and beats her breast.
WARWICK
The king I fear hath ill intreated her.
PEMBROKE
Hard is the heart that injures such a saint. 190
MORTIMER JUNIOR
I know 'tis long of Gaveston she weeps.
MORTIMER SENIOR
Why? he is gone.
MORTIMER JUNIOR   Madam, how fares your grace?
QUEEN
Ah Mortimer! now breaks the king's hate forth,
And he confesseth that he loves me not.
MORTIMER JUNIOR
Cry quittance, madam, then and love not him. 195
QUEEN
No, rather will I die a thousand deaths,
And yet I love in vain, he'll ne'er love me.

172 *Circe* Q Circes (Probably influenced by Chaucer's 'Circes' adapted
    from the French)
189 *intreated* treated

187 ff. Again the verse is formal, coming to a climax in the attribution,
    'saint', to the queen at l. 190.
195 *quittance.* A legal term denoting a release or discharge from a bond or
    obligation (cf. Hamlet's 'quietus' 'with a bare bodkin').

LANCASTER
Fear ye not, madam, now his minion's gone,
His wanton humour will be quickly left.

QUEEN
Oh never Lancaster! I am enjoined   200
To sue unto you all for his repeal;
This wills my lord, and this must I perform,
Or else be banished from his highness' presence.

LANCASTER
For his repeal, madam, he comes not back,
Unless the sea cast up his shipwrecked body.   205

WARWICK
And to behold so sweet a sight as that,
There's none here but would run his horse to death.

MORTIMER JUNIOR
But madam, would you have us call him home?

QUEEN
Ay Mortimer, for till he be restored,
The angry king hath banished me the court;   210
And therefore as thou lovest and tenderest me,
Be thou my advocate unto these peers.

MORTIMER JUNIOR
What, would ye have me plead for Gaveston?

MORTIMER SENIOR
Plead for him he that will, I am resolved.

LANCASTER
And so am I my lord; dissuade the queen.   215

QUEEN
Oh Lancaster, let him dissuade the king,
For 'tis against my will he should return.

WARWICK
Then speak not for him; let the peasant go.

QUEEN
'Tis for myself I speak and not for him.

PEMBROKE
No speaking will prevail and therefore cease.   220

MORTIMER JUNIOR
Fair queen forbear to angle for the fish,
Which being caught, strikes him that takes it dead,
I mean that vile torpedo, Gaveston,
That now I hope floats on the Irish seas.

223 *torpedo* a stinging fish (species *Torpedinidae*)

QUEEN

Sweet Mortimer, sit down by me awhile,   225
And I will tell thee reasons of such weight
As thou wilt soon subscribe to his repeal.

MORTIMER JUNIOR

It is impossible, but speak your mind.

QUEEN

Then thus, but none shall hear it but ourselves.

LANCASTER

My Lords, albeit the queen win Mortimer,   230
Will you be resolute and hold with me?

MORTIMER SENIOR

Not I against my nephew.

PEMBROKE

Fear not, the queen's words cannot alter him.

WARWICK

No? Do but mark how earnestly she pleads.

LANCASTER

And see how coldly his looks make denial.   235

WARWICK

She smiles; now for my life his mind is changed.

LANCASTER

I'll rather lose his friendship, I, than grant.

MORTIMER JUNIOR

Well, of necessity it must be so;
My lords, that I abhor base Gaveston
I hope your honours make no question,   240
And therefore though I plead for his repeal,
'Tis not for his sake, but for our avail,
Nay, for the realm's behoof and for the king's.

LANCASTER

Fie Mortimer, dishonour not thy self;
Can this be true 'twas good to banish him,   245
And is this true to call him home again?
Such reasons make white black and dark night day.

MORTIMER JUNIOR

My lord of Lancaster, mark the respect.

LANCASTER

In no respect can contraries be true.

QUEEN

Yet good my lord, hear what he can allege.   250

242 *avail* advantage
243 *behoof* benefit
248 *respect* consideration

WARWICK
  All that he speaks is nothing; we are resolved.
MORTIMER JUNIOR
  Do you not wish that Gaveston were dead?
PEMBROKE
  I would he were.
MORTIMER JUNIOR
  Why then, my lord, give me but leave to speak.
MORTIMER SENIOR
  But nephew, do not play the sophister.   255
MORTIMER JUNIOR
  This which I urge is of a burning zeal
  To mend the king and do our country good;
  Know you not Gaveston hath store of gold
  Which may in Ireland purchase him such friends
  As he will front the mightiest of us all,   260
  And whereas he shall live and be beloved,
  'Tis hard for us to work his overthrow.
WARWICK
  Mark you but that, my lord of Lancaster.
MORTIMER JUNIOR
  But were he here, detested as he is,
  How easily might some base slave be suborned,   265
  To greet his lordship with a poniard,
  And none so much as blame the murtherer,
  But rather praise him for that brave attempt,
  And in the chronicle, enroll his name
  For purging of the realm of such a plague.   270
PEMBROKE
  He saith true.
LANCASTER
  Ay, but how chance this was not done before?
MORTIMER JUNIOR
  Because my lords, it was not thought upon;
  Nay more, when he shall know it lies in us
  To banish him and then to call him home,   275
  'Twill make him vail the topflag of his pride,
  And fear to offend the meanest nobleman.
MORTIMER SENIOR
  But how if he do not, nephew?

255 *sophister* false logician
260 *front* confront, outface
276 *vail the topflag* lower his colours (with a pun on 'colour' at l. 279)

MORTIMER JUNIOR
  Then may we with some colour rise in arms,
  For howsoever we have borne it out,   280
  'Tis treason to be up against the king,
  So shall we have the people of our side,
  Which for his father's sake lean to the king;
  But cannot brook a night-grown mushrump,
  Such a one as my lord of Cornwall is,   285
  Should bear us down of the nobility,
  And when the commons and the nobles join,
  'Tis not the king can buckler Gaveston.
  We'll pull him from the strongest hold he hath;
  My lords, if to perform this I be slack,   290
  Think me as base a groom as Gaveston.
LANCASTER
  On that condition Lancaster will grant.
WARWICK
  And so will Pembroke and I.
MORTIMER SENIOR   And I.
MORTIMER JUNIOR
  In this I count me highly gratified,
  And Mortimer will rest at your command.   295
QUEEN
  And when this favour Isabel forgets,
  Then let her live abandoned and forlorn;
  But see, in happy time, my lord the king,
  Having brought the Earl of Cornwall on his way,
  Is new returned; this news will glad him much,   300
  Yet not so much as me; I love him more
  Than he can Gaveston; would he loved me
  But half so much, then were I treble blest.

              Enter KING EDWARD *mourning*

EDWARD
  He's gone, and for his absence thus I mourn;
  Did never sorrow go so near my heart   305
  As doth the want of my sweet Gaveston,
  And could my crown's revenue bring him back,

284 *mushrump* mushroom
288 *buckler* shield
289 *hold* keep, stronghold

---

303 s.d. *mourning*. The stage-direction may imply either a visible badge of
    mourning or an excessive show of grief (or both).

I would freely give it to his enemies,
And think I gained, having bought so dear a friend.
QUEEN
Hark how he harps upon his minion.   310
EDWARD
My heart is as an anvil unto sorrow,
Which beats upon it like the Cyclops' hammers,
And with the noise turns up my giddy brain,
And makes me frantic for my Gaveston;
Ah, had some bloodless Fury rose from hell,   315
And with my kingly sceptre struck me dead,
When I was forced to leave my Gaveston.
LANCASTER
Diablo, what passions call you these?
QUEEN
My gracious lord, I come to bring you news.
EDWARD
That you have parlied with your Mortimer.   320
QUEEN
That Gaveston, my lord, shall be repealed.
EDWARD
Repealed! the news is too sweet to be true.
QUEEN
But will you love me if you find it so?
EDWARD
If it be so, what will not Edward do?
QUEEN
For Gaveston but not for Isabel.   325
EDWARD
For thee fair queen, if thou lovest Gaveston,
I'll hang a golden tongue about thy neck,
Seeing thou hast pleaded with so good success.
QUEEN
No other jewels hang about my neck

---

315 *rose* risen

---

312 *Cyclops' hammers.* The Cyclops were Vulcan's workmen in his sub-
    terranean forge. The king's simile implies therefore both his darkness
    and the tragic vigour of the blows upon his heart.
327 *golden tongue.* Symbolic ornament was frequent, on and off the stage.
    One of the finest portraits of Queen Elizabeth depicts a costume of
    brocade ornamented with eyes and ears which might have been designed
    by a twentieth-century surrealist.

Than these my lord, nor let me have more wealth,   330
Than I may fetch from this rich treasury;
Oh how a kiss revives poor Isabel.

EDWARD

Once more receive my hand and let this be
A second marriage 'twixt thy self and me.

QUEEN

And may it prove more happy than the first;   335
My gentle lord, bespeak these nobles fair
That wait attendance for a gracious look,
And on their knees salute your majesty.

EDWARD

Courageous Lancaster, embrace thy king,
And as gross vapours perish by the sun,   340
Even so let hatred with thy sovereign's smile;
Live thou with me as my companion.

LANCASTER

This salutation overjoys my heart.

EDWARD

Warwick shall be my chiefest counsellor;
These silver hairs will more adorn my court,   345
Than gaudy silks or rich embroidery;
Chide me, sweet Warwick, if I go astray.

WARWICK

Slay me, my lord, when I offend your grace.

EDWARD

In solemn triumphs and in public shows
Pembroke shall bear the sword before the king.   350

PEMBROKE

And with this sword Pembroke will fight for you.

EDWARD

But wherefore walks young Mortimer aside?
Be thou commander of our royal fleet,
Or if that lofty office like thee not,
I make thee here Lord Marshal of the Realm.   355

MORTIMER JUNIOR

My lord, I'll marshal so your enemies
As England shall be quiet and you safe.

330 *these* the queen's arms   346 *embroidery* Q imbrotherie

---

349 *solemn triumphs . . . public shows.* A return, in sober key, to the theatrical
    entertainment promised by Gaveston in the opening scene.
352 ff. This whole passage, with its establishment of high offices for the
    barons, is unhistoric but highly effective dramatic invention.

EDWARD
  And as for you, Lord Mortimer of Chirk,
  Whose great achievements in our foreign war
  Deserves no common place nor mean reward: 360
  Be you the general of the levied troops,
  That now are ready to assail the Scots.
MORTIMER SENIOR
  In this your grace hath highly honoured me,
  For with my nature war doth best agree.
QUEEN
  Now is the King of England rich and strong,   365
  Having the love of his renowned peers.
EDWARD
  Ay Isabel, ne'er was my heart so light;
  Clerk of the Crown, direct our warrant forth
  For Gaveston to Ireland; Beaumont fly
  As fast as Iris or Jove's Mercury.   370
BEAUMONT
  It shall be done, my gracious lord.   [*Exit*]
EDWARD
  Lord Mortimer, we leave you to your charge;
  Now let us in and feast it royally.
  Against our friend the Earl of Cornwall comes
  We'll have a general tilt and tournament   375
  And then his marriage shall be solemnised,
  For wot you not that I have made him sure
  Unto our cousin, the Earl of Gloucester's heir.
LANCASTER
  Such news we hear, my lord.
EDWARD
  That day, if not for him, yet for my sake,   380
  Who in the triumph will be challenger,
  Spare for no cost; we will requite your love.
WARWICK
  In this or aught your highness shall command us.
EDWARD
  Thanks, gentle Warwick; come let's in and revel.   *Exeunt*

          The MORTIMERS *remain*
MORTIMER SENIOR
  Nephew, I must to Scotland; thou stayest here.   385
  Leave now to oppose thyself against the king;
  Thou seest by nature he is mild and calm,

378 *cousin* kinsman or kinswoman

And seeing his mind so dotes on Gaveston,
Let him without controlment have his will.
The mightiest kings have had their minions,   390
Great Alexander loved Hephaestion,
The conquering Hercules for Hylas wept,
And for Patroclus stern Achilles drooped:
And not kings only, but the wisest men:
The Roman Tully loved Octavius,   395
Grave Socrates, wild Alcibiades;
Then let his grace, whose youth is flexible,
And promiseth as much as we can wish,
Freely enjoy that vain light-headed earl,
For riper years will wean him from such toys.   400

MORTIMER JUNIOR

Uncle, his wanton humour grieves not me,
But this I scorn, that one so basely born
Should by his sovereign's favour grow so pert
And riot it with the treasure of the realm,
While soldiers mutiny for want of pay;   405
He wears a lord's revenue on his back,
And Midas-like he jets it in the court,
With base outlandish cullions at his heels,
Whose proud fantastic liveries make such show,
As if that Proteus, god of shapes, appeared;   410
I have not seen a dapper jack so brisk.
He wears a short Italian hooded cloak
Larded with pearl, and in his Tuscan cap
A jewel of more value than the crown;
While others walk below, the king and he   415
From out a window laugh at such as we
And flout our train and jest at our attire.
Uncle, 'tis this that makes me impatient.

392 *Hercules* Q Hector   407 *jets* struts
408 *cullions* rascals   411 *dapper jack* smart fellow
413 *Larded* covered, 'basted over'
415 *While others* Q whiles other

---

390 ff. The classical parallels from Greece and Rome, of passionate friend-
    ships place Edward's 'homosexuality' in an essentially Elizabethan con-
    text and tone. (See Introduction, pp. xvi and xxi–xxii.)
406 *wears a lord's revenue*. Elizabethan and Jacobean dramatists (notably
    Jonson, and Tourneur in *The Revenger's Tragedy*) note with reprehen-
    sion the courtly ostentation in dress which squandered lands and
    patrimony and impoverished the landed gentry.

MORTIMER SENIOR
    But nephew, now you see the king is changed.
MORTIMER JUNIOR
    Then so am I, and live to do him service,   420
    But whiles I have a sword, a hand, a heart,
    I will not yield to any such upstart.
    You know my mind; come uncle, let's away.   *Exeunt*

[Act II, Scene i]

Enter SPENCER [JUNIOR] *and* BALDOCK

BALDOCK
    Spencer,
    Seeing that our Lord th'Earl of Gloucester's dead,
    Which of the nobles dost thou mean to serve?
SPENCER JUNIOR
    Not Mortimer nor any of his side,
    Because the king and he are enemies.   5
    Baldock, learn this of me: a factious lord
    Shall hardly do himself good, much less us,
    But he that hath the favour of a king
    May with one word advance us while we live.
    The liberal Earl of Cornwall is the man,   10
    On whose good fortune Spencer's hope depends.
BALDOCK
    What! mean you then to be his follower?
SPENCER JUNIOR
    No, his companion, for he loves me well
    And would have once preferred me to the king.
BALDOCK
    But he is banished; there's small hope of him.   15
SPENCER JUNIOR
    Ay for a while, but, Baldock, mark the end:
    A friend of mine told me in secrecy,
    That he's repealed and sent for back again
    And even now a post came from the court
    With letters to our lady from the king,   20
    And as she read, she smiled, which makes me think
    It is about her lover, Gaveston.
BALDOCK
    'Tis like enough, for since he was exiled,

6 *factious* seditious

3—E II

She neither walks abroad nor comes in sight;
But I had thought the match had been broke off   25
And that his banishment had changed her mind.

SPENCER JUNIOR

Our lady's first love is not wavering;
My life for thine, she will have Gaveston.

BALDOCK

Then hope I by her means to be preferred,
Having read unto her since she was a child.   30

SPENCER JUNIOR

Then Baldock, you must cast the scholar off
And learn to court it like a gentleman;
'Tis not a black coat and a little band,
A velvet-caped cloak, faced before with serge,
And smelling to a nosegay all the day,   35
Or holding of a napkin in your hand,
Or saying a long grace at a table's end,
Or making low legs to a nobleman,
Or looking downward, with your eye-lids close,
And saying, 'truly an't may please your honour',   40
Can get you any favour with great men.
You must be proud, bold, pleasant, resolute,
And now and then stab as occasion serves.

BALDOCK

Spencer, thou knowest I hate such formal toys,
And use them but of mere hypocrisy.   45
Mine old lord while he lived was so precise,
That he would take exceptions at my buttons,
And being like pins' heads, blame me for the bigness,
Which made me curate-like in mine attire,
Though inwardly licentious enough   50
And apt for any kind of villainy.
I am none of these common pedants, I,
That cannot speak without *propterea quod*.

33 *band* white band (as a neckerchief or tie)
38 *low legs* bow, make obeisance

31–32 *scholar . . . gentleman.* Marlowe would be well informed on the
     possibilities of courtly advancement and ennoblement for the skilful
     scholar.
53–54 *propterea quod . . . quandoquidem.* Both imply stages in a scholarly
     argument ('because', 'and hence') and are therefore related to 'form a
     verb' in the next line, a translation of Quintilian's 'verba formare',
     elegant or effective rhetorical argument.

SPENCER JUNIOR
  But one of those that saith *quandoquidem*,
  And hath a special gift to form a verb.   55
BALDOCK
  Leave off this jesting, here my lady comes.

Enter the LADY [*the* KING'S NIECE]

KING'S NIECE
  The grief for his exile was not so much,
  As is the joy of his returning home.
  This letter came from my sweet Gaveston;
  What needst thou, love, thus to excuse thyself?   60
  I know thou couldst not come and visit me.
  'I will not long be from thee though I die':
  This argues the entire love of my lord,
  'When I forsake thee, death seize on my heart,'
  But rest thee here where Gaveston shall sleep.   65
  Now to the letter of my lord the king;
  He wills me to repair unto the court,
  And meet my Gaveston; why do I stay,
  Seeing that he talks thus of my marriage day?
  Who's there? Baldock,   70
  See that my coach be ready; I must hence.
BALDOCK
  It shall be done, madam.   *Exit*
KING'S NIECE
  And meet me at the park pale presently;
  Spencer, stay you and bear me company,
  For I have joyful news to tell thee of;   75
  My lord of Cornwall is a-coming over
  And will be at the court as soon as we.
SPENCER
  I knew the king would have him home again.
KING'S NIECE
  If all things sort out, as I hope they will,
  Thy service, Spencer, shall be thought upon.   80
SPENCER
  I humbly thank your ladyship.
KING'S NIECE
  Come lead the way; I long till I am there.   [*Exeunt*]

73 *pale* fence, entrance

[Act II, Scene ii]

Enter EDWARD, *the* QUEEN, LANCASTER, MORTIMER JUNIOR,
WARWICK, PEMBROKE, KENT, *attendants*

EDWARD
  The wind is good, I wonder why he stays;
  I fear me he is wrecked upon the sea.
QUEEN
  Look, Lancaster, how passionate he is,
  And still his mind runs on his minion.
LANCASTER
  My lord.   5
EDWARD
  How now, what news? is Gaveston arrived?
MORTIMER JUNIOR
  Nothing but Gaveston; what means your grace?
  You have matters of more weight to think upon;
  The King of France sets foot in Normandy.
EDWARD
  A trifle; we'll expel him when we please;   10
  But tell me, Mortimer, what's thy device
  Against the stately triumph we decreed?
MORTIMER JUNIOR
  A homely one, my lord, not worth the telling.
EDWARD
  Prithee let me know it.
MORTIMER JUNIOR
  But seeing you are so desirous, thus it is: 15
  A lofty cedar tree fair flourishing,
  On whose top-branches kingly eagles perch,
  And by the bark a canker creeps me up,
  And gets unto the highest bough of all,
  The motto: *Æque tandem.*   20

---

11 *device* painting or *impresa*

11–12 *device . . . stately triumph.* The creation of an *impresa,* a symbolic
    decoration for a masque or pageant, was a customary part of a drama-
    tist's skill—and that of a gentleman. In this passage the barons make a
    sophisticated riposte to Edward's prevailing passion for entertainment
    of this Lylyean kind.
20 *Æque tandem,* 'equal at length or in height', i.e. the 'canker' (the
    favourite) has crept to the height of the royal cedar.

EDWARD
  And what is yours, my lord of Lancaster?
LANCASTER
  My lord, mine's more obscure than Mortimer's:
  Pliny reports there is a flying-fish
  Which all the other fishes deadly hate,
  And therefore being pursued, it takes the air;   25
  No sooner is it up, but there's a fowl
  That seizeth it; this fish, my lord, I bear,
  The motto this: *Undique mors est.*
EDWARD
  Proud Mortimer, ungentle Lancaster,
  Is this the love you bear your sovereign?   30
  Is this the fruit your reconcilement bears?
  Can you in words make show of amity
  And in your shields display your rancorous minds?
  What call you this but private libelling
  Against the Earl of Cornwall and my brother?   35
QUEEN
  Sweet husband be content, they all love you.
EDWARD
  They love me not that hate my Gaveston.
  I am that cedar, shake me not too much,
  And you the eagles, soar ye ne'er so high,
  I have the jesses that will pull you down,   40
  And *Æque tandem* shall that canker cry
  Unto the proudest peer of Britainy.
  Though thou comparest him to a flying fish,
  And threatenest death whether he rise or fall,
  'Tis not the hugest monster of the sea,   45
  Nor foulest harpy that shall swallow him.
MORTIMER JUNIOR
  If in his absence thus he favours him,
  What will he do whenas he shall be present?
LANCASTER
  That shall we see; look where his lordship comes.

Enter GAVESTON

40 *jesses* strings (for a hawk)

---

23 *Pliny reports.* Pliny's *Natural History* was a regular source of dramatic
    parallels and *impresa* devices, particularly in the works of John Lyly,
    whom Marlowe appears here to be echoing.
28 *Undique mors est.* Death is on all sides.
46 *foulest harpy,* voracious birds with female heads, in classical mythology.

EDWARD
My Gaveston!   50
Welcome to Tynemouth, welcome to thy friend;
Thy absence made me droop and pine away,
For as the lovers of fair Danaë,
When she was locked up in a brasen tower,
Desired her more and waxed outrageous,   55
So did it sure with me; and now thy sight
Is sweeter far than was thy parting hence
Bitter and irksome to my sobbing heart.

GAVESTON
Sweet lord and king, your speech preventeth mine,
Yet have I words left to express my joy: 60
The shepherd nipt with biting winter's rage,
Frolics not more to see the painted spring,
Than I do to behold your majesty.

EDWARD
Will none of you salute my Gaveston?

LANCASTER
Salute him? yes; welcome Lord Chamberlain.   65

MORTIMER JUNIOR
Welcome is the good Earl of Cornwall.

WARWICK
Welcome Lord Governor of the Isle of Man.

PEMBROKE
Welcome Master Secretary.

KENT
Brother, do you hear them?

EDWARD
Still will these earls and barons use me thus?   70

GAVESTON
My lord I cannot brook these injuries.

QUEEN
Ay me, poor soul, when these begin to jar.

EDWARD
Return it to their throats; I'll be thy warrant.

GAVESTON
Base leaden earls that glory in your birth,
Go sit at home and eat your tenants' beef,   75

59 *preventeth* anticipates   62 *painted* ornamented (with flowers)

---

53 *Danaë*. Acrisius, Danaë's father, locked her in a tower to frustrate the
  prediction that her son would kill him. Perseus, her son by Jupiter, in
  fact fulfilled the prophecy.

And come not here to scoff at Gaveston,
Whose mounting thoughts did never creep so low,
As to bestow a look on such as you.
LANCASTER　　*[Draws his sword]*
Yet I disdain not to do this for you.
EDWARD
Treason, treason! where's the traitor?　　　80
PEMBROKE
Here, here.
EDWARD
Convey hence Gaveston, they'll murder him.
GAVESTON
The life of thee shall salve this foul disgrace.
MORTIMER JUNIOR
Villain, thy life, unless I miss mine aim.
[Wounds GAVESTON]
QUEEN
Ah, furious Mortimer, what hast thou done?　　　85
MORTIMER JUNIOR
No more than I would answer were he slain.
[Exit GAVESTON *with attendant]*
EDWARD
Yes, more than thou canst answer though he live.
Dear shall you both aby this riotous deed.
Out of my presence, come not near the court.
MORTIMER JUNIOR
I'll not be barred the court for Gaveston.　　　90
LANCASTER
We'll hale him by the ears unto the block.
EDWARD
Look to your own heads; his is sure enough.
WARWICK
Look to your own crown, if you back him thus.
KENT
Warwick, these words do ill beseem thy years.
EDWARD
Nay, all of them conspire to cross me thus,　　　95
But if I live, I'll tread upon their heads
That think with high looks thus to tread me down.
Come Edmund let's away, and levy men,
'Tis war that must abate these barons' pride　*Exit the* KING
[with QUEEN, KENT *and* GAVESTON]

79 *this* to attack him　　　88 *aby* atone

WARWICK
Let's to our castles, for the king is moved.   100
MORTIMER JUNIOR
Moved may he be and perish in his wrath.
LANCASTER
Cousin, it is no dealing with him now;
He means to make us stoop by force of arms,
And therefore let us jointly here protest
To prosecute that Gaveston to the death.   105
MORTIMER JUNIOR
By heaven, the abject villain shall not live.
WARWICK
I'll have his blood or die in seeking it.
PEMBROKE
The like oath Pembroke takes.
LANCASTER
And so doth Lancaster.
Now send our heralds to defy the king   110
And make the people swear to put him down.

Enter a Post

MORTIMER JUNIOR
Letters, from whence?
MESSENGER
From Scotland, my lord.
LANCASTER
Why, how now, cousin, how fares all our friends?
MORTIMER JUNIOR
My uncle's taken prisoner by the Scots.   115
LANCASTER
We'll have him ransomed, man, be of good cheer.
MORTIMER JUNIOR
They rate his ransom at five thousand pound.
Who should defray the money but the king,
Seeing he is taken prisoner in his wars?
I'll to the king.   120
LANCASTER
Do cousin, and I'll bear thee company.
WARWICK
Meantime, my lord of Pembroke and my self
Will to Newcastle here and gather head.

102 *it is no dealing* there is no . . .
104 *protest* declare, swear
123 *gather head* muster forces

MORTIMER JUNIOR
  About it then and we will follow you.
LANCASTER
  Be resolute and full of secrecy.   125
WARWICK
  I warrant you.
MORTIMER JUNIOR
  Cousin, and if he will not ransom him,
  I'll thunder such a peal into his ears,
  As never subject did unto his king.
LANCASTER
  Content, I'll bear my part; holla! who's there?   130

                    [*Enter* GUARD]

MORTIMER JUNIOR
  Ay, marry; such a guard as this doth well.
LANCASTER
  Lead on the way.
GUARD
  Whither will your lordships?
MORTIMER JUNIOR
  Whither else but to the king.
GUARD
  His highness is disposed to be alone.   135
LANCASTER
  Why, so he may, but we will speak to him.
GUARD
  You may not in my lord.
MORTIMER JUNIOR
  May we not.

                [*Enter the* KING *with* KENT]

EDWARD
  How now, what noise is this?
  Who have we there? is't you?   140
MORTIMER JUNIOR
  Nay, stay my lord, I come to bring you news,
  Mine uncle's taken prisoner by the Scots.
EDWARD
  Then ransom him.
LANCASTER
  'Twas in your wars; you should ransom him.
MORTIMER JUNIOR
  And you shall ransom him, or else . . .   145

KENT

What, Mortimer, you will not threaten him?

EDWARD

Quiet yourself; you shall have the broad seal,
To gather for him throughout the realm.

LANCASTER

Your minion Gaveston hath taught you this.

MORTIMER JUNIOR

My lord, the family of the Mortimers   150
Are not so poor but would they sell their land
Would levy men enough to anger you;
We never beg but use such prayers as these.

                              [*Drawing his sword*]

EDWARD

Shall I still be haunted thus?

MORTIMER JUNIOR

Nay, now you are here alone, I'll speak my mind.   155

LANCASTER

And so will I, and then, my lord, farewell.

MORTIMER JUNIOR

The idle triumphs, masques, lascivious shows
And prodigal gifts bestowed on Gaveston,
Have drawn thy treasure dry, and made thee weak,
The murmuring commons overstretched hath.   160

LANCASTER

Look for rebellion, look to be deposed.
Thy garrisons are beaten out of France
And lame and poor lie groaning at the gates;
The wild O'Neil, with swarms of Irish kerns,
Lives uncontrolled within the English pale;   165
Unto the walls of York the Scots made road,
And unresisted drave away rich spoils.

164 *kerns* rustic (footsoldier, pun Irish)
166 *road* inroad, raids

147 *broad seal, To gather.* The king might grant authority under his Great
    Seal to levy forces or money throughout the realm. Edward here cites
    his power ironically.
157 *idle triumphs, masques, lascivious shows,* the baronial 'plain man's' devalu-
    ation of the king's taste.
164–165 *O'Neil . . . Irish kerns . . . pale.* Marlowe is making no precise
    historic reference but uses O'Neil as a general term for an Irish leader
    of 'kerns' or foot-soldiers, led against the 'pale' or English settlement.

MORTIMER JUNIOR
   The haughty Dane commands the narrow seas,
   While in the harbour ride thy ships unrigged.
LANCASTER
   What foreign prince sends thee ambassadors?   170
MORTIMER JUNIOR
   Who loves thee but a sort of flatterers?
LANCASTER
   Thy gentle queen, sole sister to Valois,
   Complains that thou hast left her all forlorn.
MORTIMER JUNIOR
   Thy court is naked, being bereft of those
   That make a king seem glorious to the world,   175
   I mean the peers, whom thou shouldst dearly love;
   Libels are cast against thee in the street,
   Ballads and rhymes made of thy overthrow.
LANCASTER
   The northern borderers seeing the houses burnt,
   Their wives and children slain, run up and down,   180
   Cursing the name of thee and Gaveston.
MORTIMER JUNIOR
   When wert thou in the field with banner spread?
   But once, and then thy soldiers marched like players,
   With garish robes, not armour, and thyself
   Bedaubed with gold, rode laughing at the rest,   185
   Nodding and shaking of thy spangled crest,
   Where women's favours hung like labels down.
LANCASTER
   And thereof came it that the fleering Scots,
   To England's high disgrace, have made this jig:
      'Maids of England, sore may you mourn,   190
      For your lemans you have lost at Bannocksbourn,
        With a heave and a ho,
      What weeneth the King of England,
      So soon to have won Scotland?
        With a rombelow.'   195

---

171 *sort* pack   187 *labels* seal-label on a document
188 *fleering* mocking   191 *lemans* lovers

---

183 *soldiers marched like players*. The climax of the soldier-barons' contempt
    for Edward's levity and theatricality.
190 ff. The words of the jig are taken not from Holinshed but from Fabyan's
    Chronicle (1533).

MORTIMER JUNIOR
Wigmore shall fly to set my uncle free.
LANCASTER
And when 'tis gone, our swords shall purchase more;
If ye be moved, revenge it as you can,
Look next to see us with our ensigns spread.

Exeunt NOBLES

EDWARD
My swelling heart for very anger breaks;   200
How oft have I been baited by these peers
And dare not be revenged, for their power is great;
Yet shall the crowing of these cockerels
Affright a lion? Edward, unfold thy paws
And let their lives' blood slake thy fury's hunger;   205
If I be cruel and grow tyrannous,
Now let them thank themselves and rue too late.
KENT
My lord, I see your love to Gaveston
Will be the ruin of the realm and you,
For now the wrathful nobles threaten wars,   210
And therefore, brother, banish him for ever.
EDWARD
Art thou an enemy to my Gaveston?
KENT
Ay, and it grieves me that I favoured him.
EDWARD
Traitor, be gone; whine thou with Mortimer.
KENT
So will I, rather than with Gaveston.   215
EDWARD
Out of my sight and trouble me no more.
KENT
No marvel though thou scorn thy noble peers,
When I thy brother am rejected thus.   *Exit*
EDWARD
Away! poor Gaveston, that hast no friend but me,
Do what they can, we'll live in Tynemouth here,   220
And so I walk with him about the walls,
What care I though the earls begirt us round?
Here comes she that's cause of all these jars.

Enter the QUEEN, *three* LADIES [*the* KING'S NIECE *and two ladies
in waiting*, GAVESTON], BALDOCK, *and* SPENCER

QUEEN
My lord, 'tis thought the earls are up in arms.
EDWARD
Ay, and 'tis likewise thought you favour him.　　225
QUEEN
Thus do you still suspect me without cause.
KING'S NIECE
Sweet uncle speak more kindly to the queen.
GAVESTON
My lord, dissemble with her, speak her fair.
EDWARD
Pardon me, sweet, I forgot my self.
QUEEN
Your pardon is quickly got of Isabel.　　230
EDWARD
The younger Mortimer is grown so brave,
That to my face he threatens civil wars.
GAVESTON
Why do you not commit him to the Tower?
EDWARD
I dare not, for the people love him well.
GAVESTON
Why then we'll have him privily made away.　　235
EDWARD
Would Lancaster and he had both caroused
A bowl of poison to each other's health:
But let them go, and tell me what are these.
KING'S NIECE
Two of my father's servants whilst he lived;
May't please your grace to entertain them now.　　240
EDWARD
Tell me, where wast thou born? what is thine arms?
BALDOCK
My name is Baldock and my gentry
I fetched from Oxford, not from heraldry.

---

242 *gentry* rank of gentleman

242–243 *my gentry I fetched from Oxford.* A university degree carried the
right to claim a coat of arms and hence a title of gentility. Compare
Gaveston's description of Spencer below as 'well allied' (of good
family) and hence Edward's promise of a 'higher style' (nobility) than
that of gentleman 'ere long'.

EDWARD

    The fitter art thou, Baldock, for my turn;

    Wait on me, and I'll see thou shalt not want.   245

BALDOCK

    I humbly thank your majesty.

EDWARD

    Knowest thou him, Gaveston?

GAVESTON   Ay, my lord;

    His name is Spencer, he is well allied;

    For my sake let him wait upon your grace;

    Scarce shall you find a man of more desert.   250

EDWARD

    Then Spencer wait upon me; for his sake

    I'll grace thee with a higher style ere long.

SPENCER

    No greater titles happen unto me

    Than to be favoured of your majesty.

EDWARD

    Cousin, this day shall be your marriage feast,   255

    And Gaveston, think that I love thee well,

    To wed thee to our niece, the only heir

    Unto the Earl of Gloucester late deceased.

GAVESTON

    I know, my lord, many will stomach me,

    But I respect neither their love nor hate.   260

EDWARD

    The headstrong barons shall not limit me;

    He that I list to favour shall be great.

    Come, let's away, and when the marriage ends,

    Have at the rebels and their complices.   *Exeunt*

[Act II, Scene iii]

Enter LANCASTER, MORTIMER JUNIOR, WARWICK, PEMBROKE,
KENT

KENT

    My lords, of love to this our native land,

    I come to join with you and leave the king,

    And in your quarrel and the realm's behoof

    Will be the first that shall adventure life.

252 *style* title

LANCASTER
    I fear me you are sent of policy,   5
    To undermine us with a show of love.
WARWICK
    He is your brother, therefore have we cause
    To cast the worst and doubt of your revolt.
KENT
    Mine honour shall be hostage of my truth;
    If that will not suffice, farewell my lords.   10
MORTIMER JUNIOR
    Stay, Edmund; never was Plantagenet
    False of his word and therefore trust we thee.
PEMBROKE
    But what's the reason you should leave him now?
KENT
    I have informed the Earl of Lancaster.
LANCASTER
    And it sufficeth. Now, my lords, know this,   15
    That Gaveston is secretly arrived,
    And here in Tynemouth frolics with the king;
    Let us with these our followers scale the walls
    And suddenly surprise them unawares.
MORTIMER JUNIOR
    I'll give the onset.
WARWICK   And I'll follow thee.   20
MORTIMER JUNIOR
    This tattered ensign of my ancestors,
    Which swept the desert shore of that dead sea,
    Whereof we got the name of Mortimer,
    Will I advance upon this castle walls;
    Drums strike alarum, raise them from their sport,   25
    And ring aloud the knell of Gaveston.
LANCASTER
    None be so hardy as to touch the king,
    But neither spare you Gaveston nor his friends.   *Exeunt*

5 *policy* craft
8 *cast* forecast
21 *tattered* Q tottered

---

5 *policy*. Here the essentially Machiavellian word is used of Mortimer's
   devices. American usage, preserving a seventeenth-century distinction,
   still rates 'politician' as a derogatory word by contrast with 'statesman'.
22–23 *dead sea . . . Mortimer*. A false etymology. The family name is derived
   not from the Crusades but from the Normandy village of Mortemer.

[Act II, Scene iv]

Enter the KING *and* SPENCER; *to them* GAVESTON

EDWARD
  Oh tell me, Spencer, where is Gaveston?
SPENCER
  I fear me he is slain, my gracious lord.
EDWARD
  No, here he comes; now let them spoil and kill;

  [*Enter the* QUEEN, *the* KING'S NIECE, GAVESTON *and* NOBLES]

  Fly, fly, my lords, the earls have got the hold;
  Take shipping and away to Scarborough;   5
  Spencer and I will post away by land.
GAVESTON
  Oh stay, my lord; they will not injure you.
EDWARD
  I will not trust them, Gaveston; away!
GAVESTON
  Farewell, my lord.
EDWARD
  Lady, farewell.   10
KING'S NIECE
  Farewell, sweet uncle, till we meet again.
EDWARD
  Farewell, sweet Gaveston, and farewell niece.
QUEEN
  No farewell to poor Isabel, thy queen?
EDWARD
  Yes, yes, for Mortimer your lover's sake.
                              [*Exeunt all but* ISABELLA]
QUEEN
  Heavens can witness I love none but you;   15
  From my embracements thus he breaks away;
  Oh that mine arms could close this isle about,
  That I might pull him to me where I would,
  Or that these tears that drizzle from mine eyes

  17 *arms could close this isle about.* This reference to the island of Britain,
    contrasted with Edward's unconcern for its 'fleeting' on the seas,
    establishes her continuing love for the king beyond the point of his
    accusations of her infidelity with Mortimer.

Had power to mollify his stony heart,   20
That when I had him we might never part.

Enter the BARONS; *alarums*

LANCASTER
I wonder how he scaped.
MORTIMER JUNIOR   Who's this? the queen!
QUEEN
Ay, Mortimer, the miserable queen,
Whose pining heart her inward sighs have blasted
And body with continual mourning wasted;   25
These hands are tired with haling of my lord
From Gaveston, from wicked Gaveston,
And all in vain, for when I speak him fair,
He turns away and smiles upon his minion.
MORTIMER JUNIOR
Cease to lament and tell us where's the king?   30
QUEEN
What would you with the king? is't him you seek?
LANCASTER
No, madam, but that cursed Gaveston;
Far be it from the thought of Lancaster
To offer violence to his sovereign;
We would but rid the realm of Gaveston;   35
Tell us where he remains and he shall die.
QUEEN
He's gone by water unto Scarborough;
Pursue him quickly and he cannot scape;
The king hath left him and his train is small.
WARWICK
Forslow no time; sweet Lancaster, let's march.   40
MORTIMER JUNIOR
How comes it that the king and he is parted?
QUEEN
That this your army, going several ways,
Might be of lesser force, and with the power
That he intendeth presently to raise,
Be easily suppressed; and therefore be gone.   45
MORTIMER JUNIOR
Here in the river rides a Flemish hoy;
Let's all aboard and follow him amain.

40 *Forslow* hinder, waste
46 *hoy* sloop, small vessel

LANCASTER

    The wind that bears him hence will fill our sails,
    Come, come aboard, 'tis but an hour's sailing.

MORTIMER JUNIOR

    Madam, stay you within this castle here.   50

QUEEN

    No, Mortimer, I'll to my lord the king.

MORTIMER JUNIOR

    Nay, rather sail with us to Scarborough.

QUEEN

    You know the king is so suspicious,
    As if he hear I have but talked with you,
    Mine honour will be called in question,   55
    And therefore gentle Mortimer be gone.

MORTIMER JUNIOR

    Madam, I cannot stay to answer you
    But think of Mortimer as he deserves.

QUEEN

    So well hast thou deserved, sweet Mortimer
    As Isabel could live with thee for ever;   60
    In vain I look for love at Edward's hand,
    Whose eyes are fixed on none but Gaveston;
    Yet once more I'll importune him with prayers;
    If he be strange and not regard my words,
    My son and I will over into France   65
    And to the king, my brother, there complain
    How Gaveston hath robbed me of his love;
    But yet I hope my sorrows will have end
    And Gaveston this blessed day be slain.   *Exeunt*

[Act II, Scene v]

Enter GAVESTON *pursued*

GAVESTON

    Yet, lusty lords, I have escaped your hands,
    Your threats, your larums, and your hot pursuits,
    And though divorced from King Edward's eyes,
    Yet liveth Pierce of Gaveston unsurprised,
    Breathing, in hope (*malgrado* all your beards,   5

5 *malgrado all your beards* in spite of your intentions (proverbial)

59 *sweet Mortimer*. This swift transition in the queen's love, by contrast
    with l. 17 above, is characteristic of Marlowe's almost casual treatment
    of love between the sexes and its nice conduct and gradations.

That muster rebels thus against your king)
To see his royal sovereign once again.

Enter the NOBLES

WARWICK
Upon him, soldiers; take away his weapons.
MORTIMER JUNIOR
Thou proud disturber of thy country's peace,
Corrupter of thy king, cause of these broils,   10
Base flatterer, yield, and were it not for shame,
Shame and dishonour to a soldier's name,
Upon my weapon's point here shouldst thou fall
And welter in thy gore.
LANCASTER   Monster of men,
That like the Greekish strumpet, trained to arms   15
And bloody wars so many valiant knights,
Look for no other fortune, wretch, than death;
King Edward is not here to buckler thee.
WARWICK
Lancaster, why talkst thou to the slave?
Go, soldiers; take him hence, for by my sword   20
His head shall off; Gaveston, short warning
Shall serve thy turn; it is our country's cause
That here severely we will execute
Upon thy person: hang him at a bough.
GAVESTON
My lord!   25
WARWICK
Soldiers, have him away;
But for thou wert the favourite of a king,
Thou shalt have so much honour at our hands.
GAVESTON
I thank you all, my lords; then I perceive,
That heading is one, and hanging is the other,   30
And death is all.

Enter EARL OF ARUNDEL

LANCASTER
How now, my lord of Arundel?
ARUNDEL
My lords, King Edward greets you all by me.

---

15 *Greekish strumpet.* The dramatic animus against Helen in the Elizabethan theatre may be seen both in *Faustus*, where the destructive
   nature of his infatuation with her phantom ends in her title of 'para-
   mour', and in Shakespeare's *Troilus and Cressida*.

WARWICK
  Arundel, say your message.

ARUNDEL   His majesty,
  Hearing that you had taken Gaveston,   35
  Intreateth you by me, yet but he may
  See him before he dies, for why, he says,
  And sends you word, he knows that die he shall;
  And if you gratify his grace so far,
  He will be mindful of the courtesy.   40

WARWICK
  How now?

GAVESTON
  Renowned Edward, how thy name
  Revives poor Gaveston.

WARWICK   No, it needeth not,
  Arundel; we will gratify the king
  In other matters; he must pardon us in this;   45
  Soldiers, away with him.

GAVESTON
  Why, my lord of Warwick,
  Will not these delays beget my hopes?
  I know it, lords, it is this life you aim at;
  Yet grant King Edward this.   50

MORTIMER JUNIOR   Shalt thou appoint
  What we shall grant? soldiers away with him;
  Thus we'll gratify the king:
  We'll send his head by thee; let him bestow
  His tears on that, for that is all he gets
  Of Gaveston, or else his senseless trunk.   55

LANCASTER
  Not so, my lord, lest he bestow more cost,
  In burying him than he hath ever earned.

ARUNDEL
  My lords, it is his majesty's request,
  And in the honour of a king he swears,
  He will but talk with him and send him back.   60

WARWICK
  When? can you tell? Arundel no; we wot

---

37 *for why* because

---

47 Gaveston's private form of irony greatly strengthens the character which
   Marlowe delineates.

He that the care of realm remits
And drives his nobles to these exigents
For Gaveston, will, if he sees him once,
Violate any promise to possess him.   65
ARUNDEL
Then if you will not trust his grace in keep,
My lords, I will be pledge for his return.
MORTIMER JUNIOR
It is honourable in thee to offer this;
But, for we know thou art a noble gentleman,
We will not wrong thee so to make away   70
A true man for a thief.
GAVESTON
How meanst thou, Mortimer? this is over base.
MORTIMER JUNIOR
Away base groom, robber of king's renown,
Question with thy companions and thy mates.
PEMBROKE
My lord Mortimer, and you my lords each one,   75
To gratify the king's request therein,
Touching the sending of this Gaveston,
Because his majesty so earnestly
Desires to see the man before his death,
I will upon mine honour undertake   80
To carry him and bring him back again,
Provided this, that you, my lord of Arundel,
Will join with me.
WARWICK   Pembroke, what wilt thou do?
Cause yet more bloodshed? is it not enough
That we have taken him, but must we now   85
Leave him on 'had I wist' and let him go?
PEMBROKE
My lords, I will not over-woo your honours,
But if you dare trust Pembroke with the prisoner,
Upon mine oath I will return him back.
ARUNDEL
My lord of Lancaster, what say you in this?   90
LANCASTER
Why I say, let him go on Pembroke's word.
PEMBROKE
And you, lord Mortimer?

62 *remits* gives up   63 *exigents* extremities   64 *sees* seize Q
66 *trust his grace in keep* trust the king with the custody of Gaveston

MORTIMER JUNIOR
  How say you, my lord of Warwick?
WARWICK
  Nay, do your pleasures; I know how 'twill prove.
PEMBROKE
  Then give him me.   95
GAVESTON   Sweet sovereign, yet I come
  To see thee ere I die.
WARWICK [*Aside*]   Yet not perhaps,
  If Warwick's wit and policy prevail.
MORTIMER JUNIOR
  My lord of Pembroke, we deliver him you;
  Return him on your honour; sound away.
    Exeunt all but PEMBROKE, ARUNDEL, GAVESTON, [*and*
                          PEMBROKE'S *servants*]
PEMBROKE
  My lord, you shall go with me;   100
  My house is not far hence, out of the way
  A little, but our men shall go along;
  We that have pretty wenches to our wives,
  Sir, must not come so near and balk their lips.
ARUNDEL
  'Tis very kindly spoke, my lord of Pembroke;   105
  Your honour hath an adamant of power,
  To draw a prince.
PEMBROKE   So my lord. Come hither, James;
  I do commit this Gaveston to thee;
  Be thou this night his keeper; in the morning
  We will discharge thee of thy charge; be gone.   110
GAVESTON
  Unhappy Gaveston, whither goest thou now?
                          Exit with PEMBROKE'S *servants*
HORSE BOY
  My lord, we'll quickly be at Cobham.   *Exeunt*

---

106 *adamant* lodestone, magnet

---

 97 *Warwick's wit and policy*. A further attribution of stage Machiavel-
    lianism to Warwick.

[Act III, Scene i]

Enter GAVESTON *mourning, and the* EARL OF PEMBROKE'S *men*

GAVESTON
  Oh treacherous Warwick, thus to wrong thy friend!
JAMES
  I see it is your life these arms pursue.
GAVESTON
  Weaponless must I fall and die in bands;
  Oh must this day be period of my life,
  Centre of all my bliss! and ye be men,   5
  Speed to the king.

Enter WARWICK *and his company*

WARWICK
  My lord of Pembroke's men,
  Strive you no longer; I will have that Gaveston.
JAMES
  Your lordship doth dishonour to your self
  And wrong our lord, your honourable friend.   10
WARWICK
  No, James, it is my country's cause I follow.
  Go, take the villain; soldiers, come away;
  We'll make quick work; commend me to your master
  My friend, and tell him that I watched it well.
  Come, let thy shadow parley with King Edward.   15
GAVESTON
  Treacherous earl, shall I not see the king?

4 *period* stop, end   5 *and* if
15 *shadow* ghost

4–5 *this day be period of my life, Centre of all my bliss.* The term 'centre' is
  ambiguous in Elizabethan cosmology. Here it clearly implies a point of
  tragic decline, parallel with 'period (end) of my life'. In the arguments
  concerning an earth-centred or a sun-centred universe (the matter of
  the 'Copernican revolution') it was sometimes assumed that conserva-
  tive thinking clung to the earth as centre as a point of dignity for this
  realm of mankind, the place of God's incarnation. There is much more
  evidence for the contrary view that to the centre all evil drained. So
  Thomas Digges in his *Perfit Description of the Coelestiall Orbes* in 1576
  could refer to 'this little darke Starre wherein wee live'. Compare this
  passage with IV. vi, 61–62 below.
11 *my country's cause.* Though Machiavellian, the spring of Warwick's
  action is patriotic in opposing Edward's excesses.

WARWICK

The king of heaven perhaps; no other king;
Away.   *Exeunt* WARWICK *and his men, with* GAVESTON.
                                    JAMES *remains with the others*

JAMES

Come fellows, it booted not for us to strive;
We will in haste go certify our lord.   *Exeunt*   20

[Act III, Scene ii]

Enter KING EDWARD *and* SPENCER, [*and* BALDOCK] *with drums
and fifes*

EDWARD

I long to hear an answer from the barons
Touching my friend, my dearest Gaveston;
Ah Spencer, not the riches of my realm
Can ransom him; ah, he is marked to die.
I know the malice of the younger Mortimer;   5
Warwick I know is rough, and Lancaster
Inexorable, and I shall never see
My lovely Pierce, my Gaveston again;
The barons overbear me with their pride.

SPENCER

Were I King Edward, England's sovereign,   10
Son to the lovely Eleanor of Spain,
Great Edward Longshanks' issue, would I bear
These braves, this rage, and suffer uncontrolled
These barons thus to beard me in my land,
In mine own realm? my lord, pardon my speech.   15
Did you retain your father's magnanimity,
Did you regard the honour of your name,
You would not suffer thus your majesty
Be counterbuffed of your nobility.
Strike off their heads and let them preach on poles;   20
No doubt such lessons they will teach the rest,
As by their preachments they will profit much
And learn obedience to their lawful king.

EDWARD

Yea, gentle Spencer, we have been too mild,
Too kind to them, but now have drawn our sword,   25

---

12 *Great Edward Longshanks' issue.* Edward I was the type of the noble
   king of chivalry; his son and grandson in Marlowe's play are related to
   his regal qualities, in contrast and comparison.

And if they send me not my Gaveston,
We'll steel it on their crest, and poll their tops.

BALDOCK

This haught resolve becomes your majesty,
Not to be tied to their affection
As though your highness were a schoolboy still,   30
And must be awed and governed like a child.

Enter HUGH SPENCER, *an old man, father to the young* SPENCER,
with his truncheon, and soldiers

SPENCER SENIOR

Long live my sovereign, the noble Edward,
In peace triumphant, fortunate in wars.

EDWARD

Welcome, old man; comest thou in Edward's aid?
Then tell thy prince of whence and what thou art.   35

SPENCER SENIOR

Lo, with a band of bowmen and of pikes,
Brown bills and targeteers, four hundred strong,
Sworn to defend King Edward's royal right,
I come in person to your majesty,
Spencer, the father of Hugh Spencer there,   40
Bound to your highness everlastingly
For favours done in him unto us all.

EDWARD

Thy father, Spencer?

SPENCER JUNIOR   True, and it like your grace,
That pours in lieu of all your goodness shown
His life, my lord, before your princely feet.   45

EDWARD

Welcome ten thousand times, old man, again.
Spencer, this love, this kindness to thy king
Argues thy noble mind and disposition.
Spencer, I here create thee Earl of Wiltshire,
And daily will enrich thee with our favour,   50
That as the sunshine shall reflect o'er thee.

28 *haught* high, haughty (French *haut*)
37 *bills* halberd
  targeteers footsoldiers

---

33 *In peace triumphant, fortunate in wars.* Spencer Senior is here conceived
as having the prophetic quality of the old man (like John O'Gaunt at
the point of death). His characterisation of Edward has therefore a
peculiar irony here.

Beside, the more to manifest our love,
Because we hear Lord Bruce doth sell his land,
And that the Mortimers are in hand withal,
Thou shalt have crowns of us t'out-bid the barons,   55
And Spencer, spare them not, but lay it on.
Soldiers, a largesse, and thrice welcome all.

SPENCER JUNIOR
My lord, here comes the queen.

Enter the QUEEN *and her son, and* LEVUNE, *a Frenchman*

EDWARD   Madam, what news?

QUEEN
News of dishonour lord, and discontent,
Our friend Levune, faithful and full of trust,   60
Informeth us, by letters and by words,
That Lord Valois our brother, King of France,
Because your highness hath been slack in homage,
Hath seized Normandy into his hands;
These be the letters, this the messenger.   65

EDWARD
Welcome Levune; tush Sib, if this be all,
Valois and I will soon be friends again.
But to my Gaveston: shall I never see,
Never behold thee now? madam in this matter
We will employ you and your little son;   70
You shall go parley with the King of France.
Boy, see you bear you bravely to the king
And do your message with a majesty.

PRINCE
Commit not to my youth things of more weight
Than fits a prince so young as I to bear,   75
And fear not lord and father, heaven's great beams
On Atlas' shoulder shall not lie more safe
Than shall your charge committed to my trust.

QUEEN
Ah boy, this towardness makes thy mother fear
Thou art not marked to many days on earth.   80

---

57 *largesse* gift

66 *Sib* kinswoman (cf. sibling). Here used with undertones of tenderness
77 *Atlas' shoulder*. The earth was Atlas's burden. This assumption of a
    cosmic burden is the young prince's first sign of a regality which links
    him with his grandfather, Edward Longshanks.

EDWARD

    Madam, we will that you with speed be shipped
    And this our son. Levune shall follow you
    With all the haste we can dispatch him hence.
    Choose of our lords to bear you company,
    And go in peace, leave us in wars at home.   85

QUEEN

    Unnatural wars where subjects brave their king;
    God end them once! my lord I take my leave
    To make my preparation for France.   [*Exit*]

Enter LORD ARUNDEL

EDWARD

    What, lord Arundel, dost thou come alone?

ARUNDEL

    Yea, my good lord, for Gaveston is dead.   90

EDWARD

    Ah traitors, have they put my friend to death?
    Tell me, Arundel, died he ere thou camest,
    Or didst thou see my friend to take his death?

ARUNDEL

    Neither my lord, for as he was surprised,
    Begirt with weapons, and with enemies round,   95
    I did your highness' message to them all,
    Demanding him of them, entreating rather,
    And said, upon the honour of my name,
    That I would undertake to carry him
    Unto your highness and to bring him back.   100

EDWARD

    And tell me, would the rebels deny me that?

SPENCER JUNIOR

    Proud recreants!

EDWARD   Yea, Spencer, traitors all.

ARUNDEL

    I found them at the first inexorable;
    The Earl of Warwick would not bide the hearing,
    Mortimer hardly, Pembroke and Lancaster   105
    Spake least; and when they flatly had denied,
    Refusing to receive my pledge for him,

87 *end them once* immediately, once for all

85 *peace . . . wars at home.* Marlowe has intensified this ironic conjunction
    by conflating the events of 1312 when Gaveston was executed with that
    of 1322 when the quarrel with Valois took place.

The Earl of Pembroke mildly thus bespake:
'My lords, because our sovereign sends for him
And promiseth he shall be safe returned,   110
I will this undertake, to have him hence
And see him redelivered to your hands'.

EDWARD

Well, and how fortunes that he came not?

SPENCER JUNIOR

Some treason or some villainy was cause.

ARUNDEL

The Earl of Warwick seized him on his way;   115
For, being delivered unto Pembroke's men,
Their lord rode home, thinking his prisoner safe,
But ere he came, Warwick in ambush lay,
And bare him to his death, and in a trench
Strake off his head, and marched unto the camp.   120

SPENCER JUNIOR

A bloody part, flatly against law of arms.

EDWARD

Oh shall I speak or shall I sigh and die?

SPENCER JUNIOR

My lord, refer your vengeance to the sword
Upon these barons; hearten up your men.
Let them not unrevenged murther your friends;   125
Advance your standard, Edward, in the field,
And march to fire them from their starting holes.

EDWARD

[*Kneeling*] By earth, the common mother of us all,
By heaven, and all the moving orbs thereof,
By this right hand, and by my father's sword,   130
And all the honours 'longing to my crown,
I will have heads and lives for him as many
As I have manors, castles, towns, and towers.
Treacherous Warwick, traitorous Mortimer!
If I be England's king, in lakes of gore   135
Your headless trunks, your bodies will I trail,
That you may drink your fill and quaff in blood,
And stain my royal standard with the same,
That so my bloody colours may suggest
Remembrance of revenge immortally   140
On your accursed traitorous progeny,
You villains that have slain my Gaveston.

120 *Strake* struck

And in this place of honour and of trust,
Spencer, sweet Spencer, I adopt thee here,
And merely of our love we do create thee   145
Earl of Gloucester and Lord Chamberlain,
Despite of times, despite of enemies.

SPENCER JUNIOR
My lord, here is a messenger from the barons
Desires access unto your majesty.

EDWARD
Admit him near.   150

Enter the HERALD *from the barons, with his coat of arms*

HERALD
Long live King Edward, England's lawful lord!

EDWARD
So wish not they, I wis, that sent thee hither;
Thou comest from Mortimer and his complices,
A ranker rout of rebels never was.
Well, say thy message.   155

HERALD
The barons up in arms by me salute
Your highness with long life and happiness
And bid me say, as plainer to your grace,
That if without effusion of blood,
You will this grief have ease and remedy,   160
That from your princely person you remove
This Spencer, as a putrefying branch,
That deads the royal vine, whose golden leaves
Empale your princely head, your diadem,
Whose brightness such pernicious upstarts dim,   165
Say they, and lovingly advise your grace,
To cherish virtue and nobility,

145 *merely* entirely   152 *I wis* I feel sure

---

145 *merely of our love.* King Edward has been speaking of his revenge for
the death of Gaveston. This phrase emphasises that his honouring of
Spencer is unconnected with revenge and is a transference of his love
for Gaveston to a new object.

151 *lawful lord.* Marlowe loses no formal or informal opportunity to intensify
the dramatic irony of Edward's tragedy.

162–163 *putrefying branch . . . royal vine.* The sacred image of the vine,
sacramentally the symbol for a redeemed Israel (see Cranmer's exploration of Psalm 80 in his 'sermon' for Elizabeth's baptism at the end of
Shakespeare's *King Henry the Eighth*) is here characteristically applied
to England and to Edward. Compare this passage with V. i, 47 below.

And have old servitors in high esteem,
And shake off smooth dissembling flatterers;
This granted, they, their honours and their lives   170
Are to your highness vowed and consecrate.

SPENCER JUNIOR

Ah traitors, will they still display their pride?

EDWARD

Away, tarry no answer, but be gone;
Rebels! will they appoint their sovereign
His sports, his pleasures, and his company;   175
Yet ere thou go, see how I do divorce   *Embraces Spencer*
Spencer from me; now get thee to thy lords,
And tell them I will come to chastise them
For murthering Gaveston. Hie thee, get thee gone;
Edward with fire and sword follows at thy heels,   180
My lord, perceive you how these rebels swell;
Soldiers, good hearts, defend your sovereign's right,
For now, even now, we march to make them stoop.
Away.   *Exeunt*

Alarums, excursions, a great fight, and a retreat

[Act III, Scene iii]

Enter the KING, SPENCER SENIOR, SPENCER JUNIOR, *and the*
NOBLEMEN *of the king's side*

EDWARD

Why do we sound retreat? upon them, lords;
This day I shall pour vengeance with my sword
On those proud rebels that are up in arms,
And do confront and countermand their king.

SPENCER JUNIOR

I doubt it not, my lord, right will prevail.   5

SPENCER SENIOR

'Tis not amiss, my liege, for either part
To breathe a while; our men with sweat and dust
All choked well near, begin to faint for heat,
And this retire refresheth horse and man.

SPENCER JUNIOR

Here come the rebels.   10

Enter the BARONS, MORTIMER JUNIOR, LANCASTER, WARWICK, *and*
PEMBROKE [*and others*]

5 *right will prevail.* The dramatic irony intensified.

MORTIMER JUNIOR
Look Lancaster, yonder is Edward
Among his flatterers.
LANCASTER   And there let him be,
Till he pay dearly for their company.
WARWICK
And shall, or Warwick's sword shall smite in vain.
EDWARD
What, rebels, do you shrink, and sound retreat?   15
MORTIMER JUNIOR
No, Edward, no, thy flatterers faint and fly.
LANCASTER
They'd best betimes forsake thee and their trains,
For they'll betray thee, traitors as they are.
SPENCER JUNIOR
Traitor on thy face, rebellious Lancaster.
PEMBROKE
Away, base upstart, bravest thou nobles thus.   20
SPENCER SENIOR
A noble attempt and honourable deed
Is it not, trow ye, to assemble aid
And levy arms against your lawful king?
EDWARD
For which ere long their heads shall satisfy,
T'appease the wrath of their offended king.   25
MORTIMER JUNIOR
Then Edward, thou wilt fight it to the last
And rather bathe thy sword in subjects' blood
Than banish that pernicious company.
EDWARD
Ay, traitors all, rather than thus be braved,
Make England's civil towns huge heaps of stones   30
And ploughs to go about our palace gates.
WARWICK
A desperate and unnatural resolution.
Alarum to the fight! Saint George for England
And the barons' right!

---

24 *satisfy* make satisfaction

33–35 *St. George for England.* The ironic conflict made explicit, the patron
saint invoked on both the king's and the barons' side. This is Marlowe's
addition, for St. George was not adopted as patron until the reign of
Edward III.

EDWARD

    Saint George for England and King Edward's right!   35

                                          [Exeunt]

[Alarums and battle off-stage]

Enter EDWARD, *with the* BARONS, *captives*

EDWARD

    Now lusty lords, now, not by chance of war,

    But justice of the quarrel and the cause,

    Vailed is your pride; methinks you hang the heads,

    But we'll advance them, traitors; now 'tis time

    To be avenged on you for all your braves,   40

    And for the murther of my dearest friend,

    To whom right well you knew our soul was knit,

    Good Pierce of Gaveston, my sweet favourite;

    Ah rebels, recreants, you made him away.

KENT

    Brother, in regard of thee and of thy land   45

    Did they remove that flatterer from thy throne.

EDWARD

    So sir, you have spoke; away, avoid our presence;

                                      [Exit KENT]

    Accursed wretches, was't in regard of us,

    When we had sent our messenger to request

    He might be spared to come to speak with us,   50

    And Pembroke undertook for his return,

    That thou, proud Warwick, watched the prisoner,

    Poor Pierce, and headed him against law of arms,

    For which thy head shall overlook the rest,

    As much as thou in rage outwentst the rest?   55

WARWICK

    Tyrant, I scorn thy threats and menaces;

    'Tis but temporal that thou canst inflict.

LANCASTER

    The worst is death, and better die to live,

    Than live in infamy under such a king.

EDWARD

    Away with them; my lord of Winchester,   60

    These lusty leaders, Warwick and Lancaster,

    I charge you roundly, off with both their heads.

    Away!

38 *Vailed* furled
53 *headed* beheaded

WARWICK
  Farewell, vain world.
LANCASTER   Sweet Mortimer, farewell.
MORTIMER JUNIOR
  England, unkind to thy nobility,   65
  Groan for this grief; behold how thou art maimed.
EDWARD
  Go, take that haughty Mortimer to the Tower,
  There see him safe bestowed, and for the rest,
  Do speedy execution on them all; be gone.
MORTIMER JUNIOR
  What Mortimer! can ragged stony walls   70
  Immure thy virtue that aspires to heaven?
  No, Edward, England's scourge, it may not be;
  Mortimer's hope surmounts his fortune far.
                    [*The captive barons are led off*]
EDWARD
  Sound drums and trumpets, march with me my friends;
  Edward this day hath crowned him king anew.   *Exit*   75
SPENCER
  Levune, the trust that we repose in thee
  Begets the quiet of King Edward's land,
  Therefore be gone in haste, and with advice
  Bestow that treasure on the lords of France
  That therewith all enchanted like the guard   80
  That suffered Jove to pass in showers of gold
  To Danaë, all aid may be denied
  To Isabel the queen, that now in France
  Makes friends, to cross the seas with her young son,
  And step into his father's regiment.   85
LEVUNE
  That's it these barons and the subtle queen
  Long levied at.

---

65 *unkind* unnatural   70 *ragged* jagged, rough
71 *virtue* power (Italian *virtù*)

---

71 *virtue that aspires*. 'virtue' here is without moral connotation and is
   nearer the true Machiavellian *virtù*.
72 *England's scourge*. The ambiguous term, 'scourge', used of a tyrant, is a
   Marlovian commonplace. Like Cyrus, King of Persia, God's instrument
   to scourge his erring people, Tamburlaine or Edward might in their
   tyranny be regarded as a similar instrument.
81–82 *Danaë*. The implications of the myth are extended from II. ii, 53
   above.

BALDOCK   Yea, but Levune, thou seest
  These barons lay their heads on blocks together;
  What they intend the hangman frustrates clean.
LEVUNE
  Have you no doubts my lords, I'll clap so close   90
  Among the lords of France with England's gold
  That Isabel shall make her plaints in vain
  And France shall be obdurate with her tears.
SPENCER
  Then make for France amain; Levune away!
  Proclaim King Edward's wars and victories.   *Exeunt*   95

[Act IV, Scene i]

Enter KENT

KENT
  Fair blows the wind for France; blow gentle gale
  Till Edmund be arrived for England's good.
  Nature, yield to my country's cause in this.
  A brother, no, a butcher of thy friends,
  Proud Edward, dost thou banish me thy presence?   5
  But I'll to France, and cheer the wronged queen
  And certify what Edward's looseness is,
  Unnatural king, to slaughter noble men
  And cherish flatterers. Mortimer I stay
  Thy sweet escape; stand gracious, gloomy night,   10
  To his device.

Enter MORTIMER JUNIOR *disguised*

MORTIMER JUNIOR   Holla, who walketh there?
  Is't you, my lord?
KENT   Mortimer 'tis I;
  But hath thy potion wrought so happily?
MORTIMER JUNIOR
  It hath, my lord; the warders all asleep,
  I thank them, gave me leave to pass in peace.   15
  But hath your grace got shipping unto France?
KENT
  Fear it not.   *Exeunt*

90 *clap* strike (as in 'strike a bargain')

[Act IV, Scene ii]

Enter the QUEEN *and her* SON

QUEEN

  Ah boy, our friends do fail us all in France;
  The lords are cruel and the king unkind;
  What shall we do?
PRINCE　　　　　　　　Madam, return to England,
  And please my father well, and then a fig
  For all my uncle's friendship here in France.　　　　5
  I warrant you I'll win his highness quickly;
  'A loves me better than a thousand Spencers.
QUEEN

  Ah boy, thou art deceived at least in this,
  To think that we can yet be tuned together.
  No, no, we jar too far. Unkind Valois,　　　　　　·10
  Unhappy Isabel; when France rejects;
  Whither, Oh whither dost thou bend thy steps?

Enter SIR JOHN OF HAINAULT

SIR JOHN

  Madam, what cheer?
QUEEN　　　　　　　　Ah, good Sir John of Hainault,
  Never so cheerless nor so far distrest.
SIR JOHN

  I hear, sweet lady, of the king's unkindness,　　　　15
  But droop not, madam, noble minds contemn
  Despair; will your grace with me to Hainault
  And there stay time's advantage with your son?
  How say you, my lord, will you go with your friends,
  And shake off all our fortunes equally?　　　　　　20
PRINCE

  So pleaseth the queen my mother, me it likes;
  The king of England nor the court of France
  Shall have me from my gracious mother's side
  Till I be strong enough to break a staff
  And then have at the proudest Spencer's head.　　　　25
SIR JOHN

  Well said, my lord.

---

20 *shake off* cast off

---

20 *shake off*. Sir John of Hainault counsels the total risking of their future.

QUEEN
　Oh my sweet heart, how do I moan thy wrongs,
　Yet triumph in the hope of thee my joy.
　Ah, sweet Sir John, even to the utmost verge
　Of Europe or the shore of Tanaïs,   30
　Will we with thee to Hainault, so we will;
　The marquis is a noble gentleman;
　His grace, I dare presume, will welcome me.
　But who are these?

                    Enter KENT AND MORTIMER JUNIOR

KENT   Madam, long may you live
　Much happier than your friends in England do.   35
QUEEN
　Lord Edmund and lord Mortimer alive!
　Welcome to France; the news was here, my lord,
　That you were dead or very near your death.
MORTIMER JUNIOR
　Lady, the last was truest of the twain,
　But Mortimer, reserved for better hap,   40
　Hath shaken off the thraldom of the Tower
　And lives t'advance your standard, good my lord.
PRINCE
　How mean you? and the king my father lives?
　No, my lord Mortimer, not I, I trow.
QUEEN
　Not, son? why not? I would it were no worse.   45
　But gentle lords, friendless we are in France.
MORTIMER JUNIOR
　Monsieur le Grand, a noble friend of yours,
　Told us at our arrival all the news,
　How hard the nobles, how unkind the king
　Hath shewed himself; but madam, right makes room   50
　Where weapons want, and though a many friends
　Are made away, as Warwick, Lancaster,
　And others of our party and faction,
　Yet have we friends, assure your grace, in England

54 *assure your grace* be assured

───

30 *Tanaïs*. The river Don. Drayton's *Polyolbion* defines this as the boundary
　of two continents: 'Europe and Asia keep on Tanaïs either side', so that,
　like 'Ultima Thule', it is a locality of extreme distance, physically and
　emotively.
43 *the king my father*. The prince's growing authority in the awareness of
　degree and order.

Would cast up caps, and clap their hands for joy,   55
To see us there appointed for our foes.
KENT
Would all were well and Edward well reclaimed,
For England's honour, peace, and quietness.
MORTIMER JUNIOR
But by the sword, my lord, it must be deserved.
The king will ne'er forsake his flatterers.   60
SIR JOHN
My lords of England, sith the ungentle King
Of France refuseth to give aid of arms
To this distressed queen his sister here,
Go you with her to Hainault, doubt ye not
We will find comfort, money, men, and friends   65
Ere long, to bid the English king a base;
How say, young Prince, what think you of the match?
PRINCE
I think King Edward will out-run us all.
QUEEN
Nay son, not so, and you must not discourage
Your friends that are so forward in your aid.   70
KENT
Sir John of Hainault, pardon us I pray;
These comforts that you give our woeful queen
Bind us in kindness all at your command.
QUEEN
Yea, gentle brother, and the God of heaven
Prosper your happy motion, good Sir John.   75
MORTIMER JUNIOR
This noble gentleman, forward in arms,
Was born, I see, to be our anchor-hold.
Sir John of Hainault, be it thy renown

---

56 *appointed* made ready
66 *bid . . . a base* challenge to a match

---

66 *To bid the English king a base.* A punning relation of the verb *abase* and a
'run' in the game of 'Prisoner's base' in which a player was safe only so
long as he remained at his base. The ironic parallel of statecraft with
jousting or sport is frequent in Elizabethan drama (cf. the gift of tennis
balls at the opening of *King Henry the Fifth*). It is extended here in
'match' at l. 67 and 'out-run' at l. 68. It has a further ironic extension in
the next scene, l. 40 at King Edward's question concerning Sir John of
Hainault's 'leading the round', or dance.

That England's queen and nobles in distress
Have been by thee restored and comforted.   80

SIR JOHN

Madam, along, and you, my lord, with me,
That England's peers may Hainault's welcome see. *Exeunt*

[Act IV, Scene iii]

Enter the KING, ARUNDEL, *the two* SPENCERS, *with others*

EDWARD

Thus after many threats of wrathful war,
Triumpheth England's Edward with his friends,
And triumph Edward, with his friends uncontrolled.
My lord of Gloucester, do you hear the news?

SPENCER JUNIOR

What news, my lord?   5

EDWARD

Why man, they say there is great execution
Done through the realm; my lord of Arundel
You have the note, have you not?

ARUNDEL

From the lieutenant of the Tower, my lord.

EDWARD

I pray let us see it; what have we there?   10
Read it Spencer.

SPENCER *reads their names*

Why so, they barked apace a month ago,
Now, on my life, they'll neither bark nor bite.
Now sirs, the news from France; Gloucester, I trow,
The lords of France love England's gold so well,   15
As Isabel gets no aid from thence.
What now remains? have you proclaimed, my lord,
Reward for them can bring in Mortimer?

SPENCER JUNIOR

My lord, we have, and if he be in England,
'A will be had ere long, I doubt it not.   20

EDWARD

If, dost thou say? Spencer, as true as death,
He is in England's ground; our port-masters
Are not so careless of their king's command.

Enter a POST

How now, what news with thee? from whence come these?

POST

Letters, my lord, and tidings forth of France   25
To you my lord of Gloucester from Levune.

EDWARD

Read.

SPENCER JUNIOR

'My duty to your honour premised, etc. I have according
to instructions in that behalf, dealt with the King of France
his lords, and effected, that the queen all discontented and   30
discomforted, is gone, whither, if you ask, with Sir John of
Hainault, brother to the marquis, into Flanders; with them
are gone lord Edmund and the lord Mortimer, having in
their company divers of your nation, and others, and as constant report goeth, they intend to give King Edward battle   35
in England, sooner than he can look for them; this is all the
news of import.
                    Your honour's in all service, Levune.'

EDWARD

Ah, villains, hath that Mortimer escaped?
With him is Edmund gone associate?
And will Sir John of Hainault lead the round?   40
Welcome, a God's name, madam and your son,
England shall welcome you, and all your rout;
Gallop apace bright Phoebus through the sky,
And dusky night, in rusty iron car,
Between you both, shorten the time, I pray,   45
That I may see that most desired day
When we may meet these traitors in the field.
Ah, nothing grieves me but my little boy
Is thus misled to countenance their ills.
Come, friends, to Bristow, there to make us strong;   50
And winds as equal be to bring them in
As you injurious were to bear them forth.

---

40 *lead the round.* See note to IV, ii, 66 above.
43 *Gallop apace bright Phoebus.* Marlowe is constantly aware of the varying
speeds of time marked by the movements of the heavenly bodies. Compare this passage with its emotional opposite at Faustus's death: 'O
lente, lente currite noctis equi'.

[Act IV, Scene iv]

Enter the QUEEN, *her son*, PRINCE EDWARD, KENT, MORTIMER
JUNIOR *and* SIR JOHN OF HAINAULT

QUEEN
　　Now, lords, our loving friends and countrymen,
　　Welcome to England all with prosperous winds;
　　Our kindest friends in Belgia have we left,
　　To cope with friends at home; a heavy case
　　When force to force is knit and sword and glaive　　　　5
　　In civil broils makes kin and countrymen
　　Slaughter themselves in others and their sides
　　With their own weapons gored. But what's the help?
　　Misgoverned kings are cause of all this wrack,
　　And, Edward, thou art one among them all,　　　　　　10
　　Whose looseness hath betrayed thy land to spoil
　　And made the channels overflow with blood.
　　Of thine own people patron shouldst thou be,
　　But thou . . .
MORTIMER JUNIOR
　　Nay, madam, if you be a warrior　　　　　　　　　　15
　　Ye must not grow so passionate in speeches.
　　Lords, sith that we are by sufferance of heaven
　　Arrived and armed in this prince's right,
　　Here for our country's cause swear we to him
　　All homage, fealty and forwardness,　　　　　　　　20
　　And for the open wrongs and injuries
　　Edward hath done to us, his queen and land,
　　We come in arms to wreck it with the swords,
　　That England's queen in peace may repossess
　　Her dignities and honours and withal　　　　　　　　25
　　We may remove these flatterers from the king,
　　That havocs England's wealth and treasury.

20 *forwardness* readiness
23 *wreck* avenge

---

3 *Belgia*, the Netherlands (Gallia Belgica).
4–14 The most considered statement in the play of the political tensions
　　involved when a tyrant must be opposed by force. (See Introduction,
　　pp. xv–xvii). The queen places the emotional opposition most powerfully
　　in juxtaposing Edward's kingly duty as 'patron' or father of his people
　　with his own condition as a 'misgoverned king'.

SIR JOHN
Sound trumpets, my lord, and forward let us march;
Edward will think we come to flatter him.

KENT
I would he never had been flattered more.   [*Exeunt*]   30

[Act IV, Scene v]

Enter the KING, BALDOCK, *and* SPENCER JUNIOR, *flying about the
stage*

SPENCER JUNIOR
Fly, fly, my lord, the queen is over-strong,
Her friends do multiply and yours do fail;
Shape we our course to Ireland there to breathe.

EDWARD
What, was I born to fly and run away,
And leave the Mortimers conquerors behind?   5
Give me my horse and let's re-enforce our troops:
And in this bed of honour die with fame.

BALDOCK
Oh no my lord, this princely resolution
Fits not the time; away, we are pursued.   [*Exeunt*]

Enter KENT *alone, with a sword and target*

KENT
This way he fled, but I am come too late;   10
Edward, alas, my heart relents for thee.
Proud traitor Mortimer, why dost thou chase
Thy lawful king, thy sovereign with thy sword?
Vile wretch, and why hast thou, of all unkind,
Borne arms against thy brother and thy king?   15
Rain showers of vengeance on my cursed head,

---

14 *unkind* unnatural

10–27 Kent establishes similar tensions to those explored in the queen's
speech in the previous scene (see note above, IV. iv, 4–14) but his speech
is more dramatically and verbally complex. It begins in jerky irresolution
and concludes in formal alliterative patterns:

> Bristow to Longshanks' *b*lood
> Is *f*alse; be not *f*ound *s*ingle for *s*uspect;
> *P*roud Mortimer *p*ries near into thy walks

The argument is nicely weighed with the balance of near-synonyms
('unkind . . . unnatural') and of antithetic phrases marked by allitera-
tion ('Dissemble . . . diest'; 'kiss while they conspire').

Thou God, to whom in justice it belongs
To punish this unnatural revolt.
Edward, this Mortimer aims at thy life;
Oh fly him, then; but Edmund, calm this rage;   20
Dissemble or thou diest, for Mortimer
And Isabel do kiss while they conspire,
And yet she bears a face of love forsooth;
Fie on that love that hatcheth death and hate!
Edmund away. Bristow to Longshanks' blood   25
Is false; be not found single for suspect;
Proud Mortimer pries near into thy walks.

Enter the QUEEN, MORTIMER JUNIOR, *the young* PRINCE EDWARD
and SIR JOHN OF HAINAULT

QUEEN

Successful battles gives the God of kings
To them that fight in right and fear his wrath;
Since then successfully we have prevailed,   30
Thanks be heaven's great architect and you.
Ere farther we proceed, my noble lords,
We here create our well-beloved son,
Of love and care unto his royal person,
Lord Warden of the realm, and sith the fates   35
Have made his father so unfortunate,
Deal you, my lords in this, my loving lords,
As to your wisdoms fittest seems in all.

KENT

Madam, without offence if I may ask,
How will you deal with Edward in his fall?   40

PRINCE

Tell me, good uncle, what Edward do you mean?

KENT

Nephew, your father; I dare not call him king.

MORTIMER JUNIOR

My lord of Kent, what needs these questions?
'Tis not in her controlment, nor in ours,

26 *single for suspect* alone and therefore suspect

────────────────────

28–38 The mounting irony in the second half of the play is further com-
plicated in the queen's speech. Her son, made 'Lord Warden' under the
tutelage of the 'God of kings' displaces the majesty of King Edward,
now entitled simply 'his father'. This irony is given dramatic form in
the three succeeding speeches: 'Edward'... 'What Edward?'... 'I dare
not call him king'. At the same time the prince's question prepares for his
firm authority when he does in fact become king in the closing scenes.

But as the realm and parliament shall please,　　**45**
So shall your brother be disposed of.
[*Aside to the* QUEEN] I like not this relenting mood in
　　　　　　　　　　　　　　　　Edmund;

Madam, 'tis good to look to him betimes.

QUEEN
My lord, the Mayor of Bristow knows our mind.

MORTIMER JUNIOR
Yea madam, and they scape not easily　　**50**
That fled the field.

QUEEN　　　　　　　Baldock is with the king;
A goodly chancellor, is he not, my lord?

SIR JOHN
So are the Spencers, the father and the son.

KENT
This, Edward, is the ruin of the realm.

Enter RICE AP HOWELL, *and the* MAYOR OF BRISTOW, *with*
　　　　　　　SPENCER SENIOR

RICE
God save Queen Isabel and her princely son!　　**55**
Madam, the Mayor and citizens of Bristow,
In sign of love and duty to this presence,
Present by me this traitor to the state,
Spencer, the father to that wanton Spencer,
That like the lawless Catiline of Rome,　　**60**
Revelled in England's wealth and treasury.

QUEEN
We thank you all.

MORTIMER JUNIOR　　Your loving care in this
Deserveth princely favours and rewards;
But where's the king and the other Spencer fled?

RICE
Spencer the son, created Earl of Gloucester,　　**65**
Is with that smooth-tongued scholar Baldock gone,
And shipped but late for Ireland with the king.

MORTIMER JUNIOR
Some whirlwind fetch them back or sink them all;
They shall be started thence I doubt it not.

69 *started* like a wild animal

---

60 *lawless Catiline.* The conspiracy of Catiline (see Ben Jonson's treatment
　　of it) stands as the prototype of political disorder; hence the parallel
　　drawn here with the disorder which favourites (Gaveston and now the
　　Spencers) cause in the state.

PRINCE
    Shall I not see the king my father yet?   70
KENT
    [*Aside*] Unhappy's Edward, chased from England's bounds.
SIR JOHN
    Madam, what resteth, why stand ye in a muse?
QUEEN
    I rue my lord's ill fortune, but alas,
    Care of my country called me to this war.
MORTIMER JUNIOR
    Madam, have done with care and sad complaint;   75
    Your king hath wronged your country and himself
    And we must seek to right it as we may;
    Meanwhile, have hence this rebel to the block;
    Your lordship cannot privilege your head.
SPENCER SENIOR
    Rebel is he that fights against his prince,   80
    So fought not they that fought in Edward's right.
MORTIMER JUNIOR
    Take him away, he prates; you, Rice ap Howell,
    Shall do good service to her majesty,
    Being of countenance in your country here,
    To follow these rebellious runagates;   85
    We in meanwhile, madam, must take advice,
    How Baldock, Spencer, and their complices,
    May in their fall be followed to their end.   *Exeunt*

[Act IV, Scene vi]

Enter the ABBOT *and* MONKS *of Neath Abbey, the* KING, SPENCER
JUNIOR *and* BALDOCK

ABBOT
    Have you no doubt, my lord, have you no fear;
    As silent and as careful will we be
    To keep your royal person safe with us,
    Free from suspect and fell invasion
    Of such as have your majesty in chase,   5
    Your self, and those your chosen company,
    As danger of this stormy time requires.

---

72 *resteth* remains
79 *Your lordship cannot privilege* your nobility cannot save . . .
85 *runagates* renegades, deserters

EDWARD

   Father, thy face should harbour no deceit;
   Oh hadst thou ever been a king, thy heart
   Pierced deeply with sense of my distress,   10
   Could not but take compassion of my state;
   Stately and proud, in riches and in train,
   Whilom I was powerful and full of pomp,
   But what is he whom rule and empiry
   Have not in life or death made miserable?   15
   Come Spencer, come Baldock, come, sit down by me,
   Make trial now of that philosophy,
   That in our famous nurseries of arts
   Thou suckedst from Plato and from Aristotle.
   Father, this life contemplative is heaven,   20
   Oh that I might this life in quiet lead;
   But we alas are chased, and you my friends,
   Your lives and my dishonour they pursue;
   Yet gentle monks, for treasure, gold nor fee,
   Do you betray us and our company.   25

MONKS

   Your grace may sit secure, if none but we
   Do wot of your abode.

SPENCER JUNIOR

   Not one alive, but shrewdly I suspect
   A gloomy fellow in a mead below;
   'A gave a long look after us, my lord,   30
   And all the land I know is up in arms,
   Arms that pursue our lives with deadly hate.

BALDOCK

   We were embarked for Ireland, wretched we,
   With awkward winds and sore tempests driven,

---

13 *Whilom* formerly
27 *wot* know

---

13 The king's mood changes wholly in the first part of this scene to an
   assent to a characteristic *contemptus mundi*, a stoical philosophy com-
   bined with the prevailing neo-platonism of Marlowe's day. Edward thus
   expresses both aspects of the fashionable attitudes derived from the
   newly-founded Italian 'Academies', at Florence, Venice and Rome, 'our
   famous nurseries of arts': a denial of the worldly values of 'rule and
   empiry' and a revaluation of 'this life contemplative'.
29 *A gloomy fellow*. Later in the scene he becomes 'a Mower' and is both
   a living character of the countryside and a symbolic figure, Death the
   Reaper. (See Introduction, p. xx).

To fall on shore and here to pine in fear 35
Of Mortimer and his confederates.

EDWARD
Mortimer! who talks of Mortimer,
Who wounds me with the name of Mortimer,
That bloody man? Good father, on thy lap
Lay I this head, laden with mickle care, 40
Oh might I never open these eyes again,
Never again lift up this drooping head,
Oh never more lift up this dying heart!

SPENCER JUNIOR
Look up, my lord. Baldock, this drowsiness
Betides no good; here even we are betrayed. 45

Enter, with Welsh hooks, RICE AP HOWELL, *a Mower, and the*
EARL OF LEICESTER

MOWER
Upon my life, those be the men ye seek.

RICE
Fellow, enough; my lord, I pray be short,
A fair commission warrants what we do.

LEICESTER
The queen's commission, urged by Mortimer;
What cannot gallant Mortimer with the queen? 50
Alas, see where he sits and hopes unseen
T'escape their hands that seek to reave his life;
Too true it is, *quem dies vidit veniens superbum,*
Hunc dies vidit fugiens iacentem.
But Leicester, leave to grow so passionate; 55
Spencer and Baldock, by no other names
I arrest you of high treason here;
Stand not on titles, but obey the arrest;
'Tis in the name of Isabel the queen.
My lord, why droop you thus? 60

40 *mickle* much
52 *reave* destroy, bereave

---

45 s.d. *Welsh hooks,* bill-hooks with a cross-piece below the blade; compare
1 Henry IV, II. iv, 372, 'swore the devil his liegeman on the cross of a
Welsh hook'.
53–54 *quem dies . . . iacentem,* quoted from Seneca, *Thyestes,* 613–614. Ben
Jonson gives a rendering in the last two lines of *Sejanus* (1603):

> For whom the morning saw so great and high,
> Then low and little 'fore the even doth lie.

EDWARD
    Oh day, the last of all my bliss on earth,
    Centre of all misfortune! Oh my stars!
    Why do you lour unkindly on a king?
    Comes Leicester then in Isabella's name,
    To take my life, my company from me?   65
    Here man, rip up this panting breast of mine
    And take my heart in rescue of my friends.
RICE
    Away with them.
SPENCER JUNIOR   It may become thee yet,
    To let us take our farewell of his grace.
ABBOT
    My heart with pity yearns to see this sight,   70
    A king to bear these words and proud commands.
EDWARD
    Spencer, ah sweet Spencer, thus then must we part.
SPENCER JUNIOR
    We must, my lord, so will the angry heavens.
EDWARD
    Nay, so will hell and cruel Mortimer;
    The gentle heavens have not to do in this.   75
BALDOCK
    My lord, it is in vain to grieve or storm;
    Here humbly of your grace we take our leaves;
    Our lots are cast, I fear me so is thine.
EDWARD
    In heaven we may, in earth never shall we meet,
    And Leicester say, what shall become of us?   80
LEICESTER
    Your majesty must go to Killingworth.
EDWARD
    Must! 'tis somewhat hard, when kings must go.
LEICESTER
    Here is a litter ready for your grace,
    That waits your pleasure, and the day grows old.
RICE
    As good be gone as stay and be benighted.   85
EDWARD
    A litter hast thou? lay me in a hearse,

63 *lour unkindly* frown unnaturally

61–62 *bliss on earth, Centre of all misfortune.* See the note to III. i, 4–5.

And to the gates of hell convey me hence;
Let Pluto's bells ring out my fatal knell,
And hags howl for my death at Charon's shore,
For friends hath Edward none, but these, and these,   90
And these must die under a tyrant's sword.

RICE

My lord, be going; care not for these,
For we shall see them shorter by the heads.

EDWARD

Well, that shall be, shall be; part we must,
Sweet Spencer, gentle Baldock, part we must;   95
Hence feigned weeds, unfeigned are my woes.
Father, farewell; Leicester, thou stayest for me,
And go I must; life, farewell, with my friends.

Exeunt EDWARD *and* LEICESTER

SPENCER JUNIOR

Oh is he gone? is noble Edward gone,
Parted from hence, never to see us more?   100
Rent, sphere of heaven, and fire, forsake thy orb,
Earth melt to air, gone is my sovereign,
Gone, gone alas, never to make return.

BALDOCK

Spencer, I see our souls are fleeted hence,
We are deprived the sunshine of our life.   105
Make for a new life, man, throw up thy eyes,
And heart and hand to heaven's immortal throne,
Pay nature's debt with cheerful countenance;
Reduce we all our lessons unto this:
To die, sweet Spencer, therefore live we all,   110
Spencer, all live to die, and rise to fall.

RICE

Come, come, keep these preachments till you come to the
place appointed; You, and such as you are, have made wise
work in England. Will your lordships away?

MOWER

Your worship I trust will remember me?   115

RICE

Remember thee, fellow? what else? Follow me to the town.

[*Exeunt*]

[Act V, Scene i]

Enter the KING, LEICESTER, *with the* BISHOP OF WINCHESTER *and*
TRUSSEL *for the crown*

LEICESTER

Be patient, good my lord, cease to lament;
Imagine Killingworth Castle were your court,
And that you lay for pleasure here a space,
Not of compulsion or necessity.

EDWARD

Leicester, if gentle words might comfort me,   5
Thy speeches long ago had eased my sorrows,
For kind and loving hast thou always been.
The griefs of private men are soon allayed
But not of kings; the forest deer being struck
Runs to an herb that closeth up the wounds   10
But when the imperial lion's flesh is gored
He rends and tears it with his wrathful paw
[And] highly scorning that the lowly earth
Should drink his blood, mounts up into the air;
And so it fares with me, whose dauntless mind   15
The ambitious Mortimer would seek to curb
And that unnatural queen, false Isabel,
That thus hath pent and mewed me in a prison;
For such outrageous passions cloy my soul
As with the wings of rancour and disdain   20
Full often am I soaring up to heaven
To plain me to the gods against them both;
But when I call to mind I am a king,
Methinks I should revenge me of the wrongs
That Mortimer and Isabel have done.   25
But what are kings when regiment is gone
But perfect shadows in a sunshine day?
My nobles rule, I bear the name of king;
I wear the crown but am controlled by them,
By Mortimer and my unconstant queen,   30
Who spots my nuptial bed with infamy,
Whilst I am lodged within this cave of care,
Where sorrow at my elbow still attends

22 *plain* complain   26 *regiment* rule, power

9–12 *forest deer being struck.* Marlowe would be familiar with this lore
from Vergil, *Aeneid*, XII, 412–415, concerning the herb, dittany.

To company my heart with sad laments,
That bleeds within me for this strange exchange.   35
But tell me, must I now resign my crown
To make usurping Mortimer a king?

BISHOP OF WINCHESTER
Your grace mistakes; it is for England's good,
And princely Edward's right we crave the crown.

EDWARD
No, 'tis for Mortimer, not Edward's head,   40
For he's a lamb encompassed by wolves
Which in a moment will abridge his life;
But if proud Mortimer do wear this crown,
Heavens turn it to a blaze of quenchless fire,
Or, like the snaky wreath of Tisiphon,   45
Engirt the temples of his hateful head;
So shall not England's vines be perished,
But Edward's name survives, though Edward dies.

LEICESTER
My lord, why waste you thus the time away?
They stay your answer; will you yield your crown?   50

EDWARD
Ah Leicester, weigh how hardly I can brook
To lose my crown and kingdom without cause,
To give ambitious Mortimer my right,
That like a mountain overwhelms my bliss,
In which extreme my mind here murthered is.   55
But what the heavens appoint I must obey;
Here, take my crown, the life of Edward too,
Two kings in England cannot reign at once;
But stay awhile, let me be king till night,
That I may gaze upon this glittering crown,   60
So shall my eyes receive their last content,
My head, the latest honour due to it,
And jointly both yield up their wished right.
Continue ever thou celestial sun,
Let never silent night possess this clime;   65
Stand still you watches of the element,
All times and seasons rest you at a stay,
That Edward may be still fair England's king.
But day's bright beams doth vanish fast away,

45 *snaky wreath of Tisiphon.* Tisiphone was one of the Furies.
47 *England's vines.* See note to III. ii, 162–163.
66 *Stand still . . . element.* See note to IV. iii, 43.

And needs I must resign my wished crown;   70
Inhuman creatures, nursed with tiger's milk,
Why gape you for your sovereign's overthrow?
My diadem I mean and guiltless life;
See, monsters, see, I'll wear my crown again;
What, fear you not the fury of your king?   75
But hapless Edward, thou art fondly led;
They pass not for thy frowns as late they did,
But seek to make a new-elected king,
Which fills my mind with strange despairing thoughts,
Which thoughts are martyred with endless torments,   80
And in this torment comfort find I none,
But that I feel the crown upon my head,
And therefore let me wear it yet awhile.

TRUSSEL

My lord, the parliament must have present news,
And therefore say, will you resign or no?   85

The KING rageth

EDWARD

I'll not resign, but whilst I live
Traitors begone, and join you with Mortimer,
Elect, conspire, install, do what you will,
Their blood and yours shall seal these treacheries.

BISHOP OF WINCHESTER

This answer we'll return, and so farewell.   90

LEICESTER

Call them again, my lord, and speak them fair,
For if they go the prince shall lose his right.

EDWARD

Call thou them back; I have no power to speak.

LEICESTER

My lord, the king is willing to resign.

BISHOP OF WINCHESTER

If he be not, let him choose.   95

EDWARD

Oh would I might; but heavens and earth conspire
To make me miserable; here receive my crown;
Receive it? no, these innocent hands of mine
Shall not be guilty of so foul a crime;
He of you all that most desires my blood   100
And will be called the murtherer of a king
Take it; what, are you moved? pity you me?

76 *fondly* foolishly   77 *pass not for* do not care

Then send for unrelenting Mortimer
And Isabel, whose eyes being turned to steel,
Will sooner sparkle fire than shed a tear.   105
Yet stay, for rather than I will look on them,
Here, here! [*Resigns the crown*] now, sweet God of heaven
Make me despise this transitory pomp
And sit for aye enthronised in heaven;
Come death, and with thy fingers close my eyes,   110
Or if I live, let me forget my self.

BISHOP OF WINCHESTER
My lord . . .

EDWARD
Call me not lord; Away! out of my sight!
Ah, pardon me, grief makes me lunatic.
Let not that Mortimer protect my son;   115
More safety is there in a tiger's jaws
Than his embracements. Bear this to the queen,

                              [*Gives a handkerchief*]

Wet with my tears and dried again with sighs;
If with the sight thereof she be not moved,
Return it back and dip it in my blood;   120
Commend me to my son, and bid him rule
Better than I; yet how have I transgressed
Unless it be with too much clemency?

TRUSSEL
And thus most humbly do we take our leave.

            [*Exeunt* TRUSSEL *and* BISHOP OF WINCHESTER]

EDWARD
Farewell. I know the next news that they bring   125
Will be my death, and welcome shall it be;
To wretched men death is felicity.

                        Enter BERKELEY

LEICESTER
Another post; what news brings he?

EDWARD
Such news as I expect; come, Berkeley, come,
And tell thy message to my naked breast.   130

BERKELEY
My lord, think not a thought so villainous
Can harbour in a man of noble birth.
To do your highness service and devoir,
And save you from your foes, Berkeley would die.

LEICESTER
  My lord, the council of the queen commands   135
  That I resign my charge.
EDWARD
  And who must keep me now, must you my lord?
BERKELEY
  Ay, my most gracious lord, so 'tis decreed.
EDWARD
  By Mortimer, whose name is written here;
  Well may I rent his name that rends my heart.   140

           [Tears the paper]

  This poor revenge hath something eased my mind,
  So may his limbs be torn as is this paper;
  Hear me, immortal Jove, and grant it too.
BERKELEY
  Your grace must hence with me to Berkeley straight.
EDWARD
  Whither you will; all places are alike   145
  And every earth is fit for burial.
LEICESTER
  Favour him, my lord, as much as lieth in you.
BERKELEY
  Even so betide my soul as I use him.
EDWARD
  Mine enemy hath pitied my estate
  And that's the cause that I am now removed.   150
BERKELEY
  And thinks your grace that Berkeley will be cruel?
EDWARD
  I know not, but of this am I assured
  That death ends all and I can die but once.
  Leicester, farewell.
LEICESTER
  Not yet, my lord; I'll bear you on your way.   *Exeunt*   155

[Act V, Scene ii]

Enter MORTIMER JUNIOR *and* QUEEN ISABEL

MORTIMER JUNIOR
  Fair Isabel, now have we our desire;
  The proud corrupters of the light-brained king
  Have done their homage to the lofty gallows,
  And he himself lies in captivity.

Be ruled by me and we will rule the realm;   5
In any case, take heed of childish fear,
For now we hold an old wolf by the ears,
That if he slip will seize upon us both
And gripe the sorer being griped himself.
Think therefore, madam, that imports us much   10
To erect your son with all the speed we may
And that I be protector over him,
For our behoof will bear the greater sway
Whenas a king's name shall be under-writ.

QUEEN

Sweet Mortimer, the life of Isabel,   15
Be thou persuaded that I love thee well
And therefore, so the prince my son be safe,
Whom I esteem as dear as these mine eyes,
Conclude against his father what thou wilt
And I myself will willingly subscribe.   20

MORTIMER JUNIOR

First would I hear news that he were deposed
And then let me alone handle him.

Enter MESSENGER

MORTIMER JUNIOR

Letters, from whence?

MESSENGER   From Killingworth, my lord.

QUEEN

How fares my lord the king?

MESSENGER

In health, madam, but full of pensiveness.   25

QUEEN

Alas, poor soul, would I could ease his grief;

[*Enter the* BISHOP OF WINCHESTER *with the crown*]

Thanks, gentle Winchester; sirra, be gone.

[*Exit* MESSENGER]

WINCHESTER

The king hath willingly resigned his crown.

QUEEN

Oh happy news; send for the prince my son.

WINCHESTER

Further, ere this letter was sealed, Lord Berkeley came,   30
So that he now is gone from Killingworth,
And we have heard that Edmund laid a plot
To set his brother free; no more but so.

The lord of Berkeley is so pitiful
As Leicester that had charge of him before.   35
QUEEN
Then let some other be his guardian.
MORTIMER JUNIOR
Let me alone, here is the privy seal.
                         [*Exit the* BISHOP OF WINCHESTER]
Who's there? call hither Gurney and Matrevis.
To dash the heavy-headed Edmund's drift,
Berkeley shall be discharged, the king removed,   40
And none but we shall know where he lieth.
QUEEN
But Mortimer, as long as he survives
What safety rests for us or for my son?
MORTIMER JUNIOR
Speak, shall he presently be dispatched and die?
QUEEN
I would he were, so it were not by my means.   45

                  Enter MATREVIS *and* GURNEY

MORTIMER JUNIOR
Enough.
Matrevis, write a letter presently
Unto the lord of Berkeley from our self,
That he resign the king to thee and Gurney,
And when 'tis done, we will subscribe our name.   50
MATREVIS
It shall be done, my lord.
MORTIMER JUNIOR   Gurney.
GURNEY   My lord.
MORTIMER JUNIOR
As thou intendest to rise by Mortimer,
Who now makes Fortune's wheel turn as he please,
Seek all the means thou canst to make him droop,
And neither give him kind word nor good look.   55
GURNEY
I warrant you, my lord.
MORTIMER JUNIOR
And this above the rest, because we hear

---

53 *Fortune's wheel.* Marlowe is as ambivalent as all his contemporaries on
   the relation between his great figures and the power of Fortune.
   Tamburlaine claims to control her wheel but is subject to her vagaries;
   so Mortimer claims her to control his own destiny.

That Edmund casts to work his liberty,
Remove him still from place to place by night,
And at the last he come to Killingworth,   60
And then from thence to Berkeley back again;
And by the way to make him fret the more,
Speak curstly to him, and in any case
Let no man comfort him if he chance to weep
But amplify his grief with bitter words.   65

MATREVIS
Fear not, my lord, we'll do as you command.

MORTIMER JUNIOR
So now away, post thitherwards amain.

QUEEN
Whither goes this letter? to my lord the king?
Commend me humbly to his majesty
And tell him that I labour all in vain   70
To ease his grief and work his liberty;
And bear him this as witness of my love.

MATREVIS
I will, madam.   *Exeunt* MATREVIS *and* GURNEY

Enter the young PRINCE EDWARD, *and the* EARL OF KENT *talking
with him*

MORTIMER JUNIOR
Finely dissembled; do so still, sweet queen.
Here comes the young prince, with the Earl of Kent.   75

QUEEN
Something he whispers in his childish ears.

MORTIMER JUNIOR
If he have such access unto the prince,
Our plots and stratagems will soon be dashed.

QUEEN
Use Edmund friendly as if all were well.

MORTIMER JUNIOR
How fares my honourable lord of Kent?   80

KENT
In health, sweet Mortimer; how fares your grace?

QUEEN
Well, if my lord your brother were enlarged.

58 *casts* plans
82 *enlarged* released (with an ironic pun on 'magnified')

---

82 *enlarged*, a particular instance of Marlowe's punning irony: the king
can be enlarged (released) either by discharge from prison or death.

KENT
I hear of late he hath deposed himself.

QUEEN
The more my grief.

MORTIMER JUNIOR And mine.

KENT [*Aside*] Ah, they do dissemble.

QUEEN
Sweet son, come hither, I must talk with thee. 85

MORTIMER JUNIOR
Thou being his uncle and the next of blood
Do look to be protector over the prince.

KENT
Not I, my lord; who should protect the son
But she that gave him life, I mean the queen?

PRINCE
Mother, persuade me not to wear the crown; 90
Let him be king, I am too young to reign.

QUEEN
But be content, seeing 'tis his highness' pleasure.

PRINCE
Let me but see him first and then I will.

KENT
Ay, do, sweet nephew.

QUEEN
Brother, you know it is impossible. 95

PRINCE
Why, is he dead?

QUEEN
No, God forbid.

KENT
I would those words proceeded from your heart.

MORTIMER JUNIOR
Inconstant Edmund, dost thou favour him
That wast a cause of his imprisonment? 100

KENT
The more cause have I now to make amends.

MORTIMER JUNIOR
I tell thee 'tis not meet that one so false
Should come about the person of a prince;
My lord, he hath betrayed the king his brother
And therefore trust him not. 105

PRINCE
But he repents and sorrows for it now.

QUEEN

Come son, and go with this gentle lord and me.

PRINCE

With you I will but not with Mortimer.

MORTIMER JUNIOR

Why youngling, 's'dainst thou so of Mortimer?
Then I will carry thee by force away.   110

PRINCE

Help, uncle Kent! Mortimer will wrong me.

QUEEN

Brother Edmund, strive not; we are his friends.
Isabel is nearer than the Earl of Kent.

KENT

Sister, Edward is my charge; redeem him.

QUEEN

Edward is my son, and I will keep him.   115

KENT

Mortimer shall know that he hath wronged me.
Hence will I haste to Killingworth Castle
And rescue aged Edward from his foes,
To be revenged on Mortimer and thee.   [*Exeunt*]

[Act V, Scene iii]

Enter MATREVIS *and* GURNEY *with the* KING

MATREVIS

My lord, be not pensive, we are your friends;
Men are ordained to live in misery,
Therefore come; dalliance dangereth our lives.

EDWARD

Friends, whither must unhappy Edward go?
Will hateful Mortimer appoint no rest?   5
Must I be vexed like the nightly bird,
Whose sight is loathsome to all winged fowls?
When will the fury of his mind assuage?
When will his heart be satisfied with blood?
If mine will serve, unbowel straight this breast,   10

---

118 *aged Edward*. Edward II was in fact only forty-three at his death. (cf.
  'old Edward' at V. iii, 23 below and 'old wolf' at l. 7 above).

And give my heart to Isabel and him;
It is the chiefest mark they level at.

GURNEY

Not so, my liege, the queen hath given this charge,
To keep your grace in safety;
Your passions make your dolours to increase. 15

EDWARD

This usage makes my misery increase.
But can my air of life continue long
When all my senses are annoyed with stench?
Within a dungeon England's king is kept,
Where I am starved for want of sustenance; 20
My daily diet is heart-breaking sobs,
That almost rents the closet of my heart;
Thus lives old Edward not relieved by any,
And so must die, though pitied by many.
Oh water, gentle friends, to cool my thirst 25
And clear my body from foul excrements.

MATREVIS

Here's channel water, as our charge is given;
Sit down, for we'll be barbers to your grace.

EDWARD

Traitors away, what, will you murther me,
Or choke your sovereign with puddle water? 30

GURNEY

No, but wash your face and shave away your beard,
Lest you be known and so be rescued.

---

12 *mark they level at* target they aim at
27 *channel* ditch, drain

---

17 *air of life*, a formal, latinate phrase for 'drawing breath'.
27 *channel water*. This has been prepared for as early as I. i, 188, 'And in
the channel christen him anew', and there is evidence throughout the
scene of Marlowe's skilful and meticulous craftsmanship. The incident
is not in the prime source, Holinshed, but in Stow: 'Devising to disfigure him that hee might not bee knowne', is taken directly into
Marlowe's text; 'a little water which ranne in a ditch' becomes, here
and in Act I, 'channel water'; but the over-emotional symbolism of
Stow is modified by Marlowe: 'he would have warme water for his
beard; and, to the ende that he might keepe his promise, he began to
weepe'. This is omitted from the passage and is hinted only in the pre-
ceding lines (21–22) 'My daily diet is heart-breaking sobs, That almost
rents the closet of my heart'. Marlowe's account is terser and more
tragic, with a sardonic tone which underlines the nature of the tragic
humiliation.

MATREVIS

    Why strive you thus, your labour is in vain?

EDWARD

    The wren may strive against the lion's strength.

    But all in vain, so vainly do I strive   35

    To seek for mercy at a tyrant's hand.

They wash him with puddle water, and shave his beard away

    Immortal powers, that knows the painful cares

    That waits upon my poor distressed soul,

    Oh level all your looks upon these daring men,

    That wrongs their liege and sovereign, England's king.   40

    Oh Gaveston, it is for thee that I am wronged;

    For me both thou and both the Spencers died,

    And for your sakes a thousand wrongs I'll take.

    The Spencers' ghosts, wherever they remain,

    Wish well to mine; then tush! for them I'll die.   45

MATREVIS

    'Twixt theirs and yours shall be no enmity;

    Come, come, away; now put the torches out;

    We'll enter in by darkness to Killingworth.

Enter the EARL OF KENT

GURNEY

    How now, who comes there?

MATREVIS

    Guard the king sure, it is the Earl of Kent.   50

EDWARD

    Oh gentle brother, help to rescue me.

MATREVIS

    Keep them asunder, thrust in the king.

KENT

    Soldiers, let me but talk to him one word.

GURNEY

    Lay hands upon the earl for this assault.

KENT

    Lay down your weapons; traitors, yield the king.   55

MATREVIS

    Edmund, yield thou thyself or thou shalt die.

KENT

    Base villains, wherefore do you gripe me thus?

GURNEY

    Bind him and so convey him to the court.

KENT
    Where is the court but here, here is the king,
    And I will visit him, why stay you me?   60
MATREVIS
    The court is where Lord Mortimer remains,
    Thither shall your honour go and so farewell.
              Exeunt MATREVIS *and* GURNEY, *with the* KING

KENT
    Oh miserable is that commonweal where lords
    Keep courts, and kings are locked in prison!

              [Enter soldiers]

SOLDIERS
    Wherefore stay we? on, sirs, to the court.   65
KENT
    Ay, lead me whither you will, even to my death,
    Seeing that my brother cannot be released.   *[Exeunt]*

[Act V, Scene iv]

Enter MORTIMER JUNIOR *alone*

MORTIMER JUNIOR
    The king must die or Mortimer goes down;
    The commons now begin to pity him,
    Yet he that is the cause of Edward's death
    Is sure to pay for it when his son is of age,
    And therefore will I do it cunningly.   5
    This letter written by a friend of ours
    Contains his death yet bids them save his life.
    '*Edwardum occidere nolite timere bonum est*':
    'Fear not to kill the king, 'tis good he die.'
    But read it thus, and that's another sense: 10
    '*Edwardum occidere nolite timere bonum est*':
    'Kill not the king, 'tis good to fear the worst'.
    Unpointed as it is, thus shall it go,
    That being dead, if it chance to be found,

13 *Unpointed* unpunctuated (now used only for ecclesiastical music,
    the 'pointing of psalms')

---

59 *Where is the court but here?* The essentially personal nature of the king's
    rule is important, and all power, including that of the judges, emanates
    from the royal presence in his court. (See Introduction, p. xviii.) There
    is thus a quality of both treachery and near-blasphemy in the reply of
    Matrevis: 'The court is where Lord Mortimer remains'.

Matrevis and the rest may bear the blame,   15
And we be quit that caused it to be done;
Within this room is locked the messenger
That shall convey it and perform the rest,
And by a secret token that he bears
Shall he be murdered when the deed is done.   20
Lightborn, come forth;
Art thou as resolute as thou wast?

[*Enter* LIGHTBORN]

LIGHTBORN
What else, my lord? and far more resolute.
MORTIMER JUNIOR
And hast thou cast how to accomplish it?
LIGHTBORN
Ay, ay, and none shall know which way he died.   25
MORTIMER JUNIOR
But at his looks, Lightborn, thou wilt relent.
LIGHTBORN
Relent, ha, ha! I use much to relent!
MORTIMER JUNIOR
Well, do it bravely and be secret.
LIGHTBORN
You shall not need to give instructions;
'Tis not the first time I have killed a man;   30
I learned in Naples how to poison flowers,
To strangle with a lawn thrust through the throat,
To pierce the wind-pipe with a needle's point,
Or whilst one is asleep, to take a quill
And blow a little powder in his ears,   35
Or open his mouth and pour quicksilver down,
But yet I have a braver way than these.
MORTIMER JUNIOR
What's that?
LIGHTBORN
Nay, you shall pardon me, none shall know my tricks.

---

21 *Lightborn, come forth.* It has been suggested by Professor Harry Levin
   that Lightborn is a late reflection of the morality tradition, in that his
   name is a 'translation' of Lucifer, the fallen angel. The passages where
   Mephistophiles recollects the fall of the angels with Lucifer are a
   significant background to the demonic quality of this present character
   who does not appear in the chronicle sources. (See Introduction, p. xiii.)
30–35 Lightborn's skills are those of the Italianate Machiavel.

MORTIMER JUNIOR
> I care not how it is so it be not spied;   40
> Deliver this to Gurney and Matrevis;   [*Gives letter*]
> At every ten miles' end thou hast a horse.
> Take this, away, and never see me more.

LIGHTBORN
> No?

MORTIMER JUNIOR
> No, unless thou bring me news of Edward's death.   45

LIGHTBORN
> That will I quickly do; farewell, my lord.   [*Exit* LIGHTBORN]

MORTIMER JUNIOR
> The prince I rule, the queen do I command,
> And with a lowly congé to the ground
> The proudest lords salute me as I pass;
> I seal, I cancel, I do what I will;   50
> Feared am I more than loved, let me be feared,
> And when I frown make all the court look pale.
> I view the prince with Aristarchus' eyes,
> Whose looks were as a breeching to a boy;
> They thrust upon me the Protectorship   55
> And sue to me for that that I desire,
> While at the council-table, grave enough
> And not unlike a bashful Puritan,
> First I complain of imbecility,
> Saying it is, *onus quam gravissimum*,   60
> Till being interrupted by my friends,
> *Suscepi* that *provinciam* as they term it,
> And to conclude, I am Protector now;
> Now is all sure, the queen and Mortimer
> Shall rule the realm, the king, and none rule us;   65

---

48 *congé* bow   59 *imbecility* unfitness

---

47 ff. As the play draws to its close all the protagonists are given extended
   expositions. Mortimer here has greatly developed from the rough,
   straightforward baron of the early scenes.

53 *Aristarchus' eyes*, an early grammarian and educationist of the second
   century B.C.

60 *onus quam gravissimum*, 'a heavy load', preparing for the technical legal
   term from Roman practice, 'suscepi provinciam', 'I undertook the
   charge'. Mortimer's pride is shown at its height in the quotation from
   Ovid's *Metamorphoses* (VI, 195), 'Major sum quam cui possit fortuna
   nocere, which Golding translates (248–249) 'I am greater than that
   frowarde fortune may Empeache me'.

Mine enemies will I plague, my friends advance,
And what I list command, who dare control?
Maior sum quam cui possit fortuna nocere,
And that this be the coronation day
It pleaseth me and Isabel the queen.   70
The trumpets sound, I must go take my place.

Enter the young KING, BISHOP OF CANTERBURY, CHAMPION,
NOBLES, QUEEN

BISHOP

Long live King Edward, by the grace of God
King of England and Lord of Ireland.

CHAMPION

If any Christian, Heathen, Turk, or Jew,
Dares but affirm that Edward's not true king   75
And will avouch his saying with the sword,
I am the Champion that will combat him.

MORTIMER JUNIOR

None comes, sound trumpets.

KING

Champion, here's to thee.

QUEEN

Lord Mortimer, now take him to your charge.   80

Enter SOLDIERS *with the* EARL OF KENT *prisoner*

MORTIMER JUNIOR

What traitor have we there with blades and bills?

SOLDIER

Edmund the Earl of Kent.

KING   What hath he done?

SOLDIER

'A would have taken the king away perforce
As we were bringing him to Killingworth.

MORTIMER JUNIOR

Did you attempt his rescue, Edmund! speak.   85

KENT

Mortimer, I did; he is our king,
And thou compelst this prince to wear the crown.

MORTIMER JUNIOR

Strike off his head! he shall have martial law.

KENT

Strike off my head? base traitor, I defy thee.

KING

My lord, he is my uncle and shall live.   90

MORTIMER JUNIOR
  My lord, he is your enemy and shall die.
KENT
  Stay villains.
KING
  Sweet mother, if I cannot pardon him,
  Entreat my lord Protector for his life.
QUEEN
  Son, be content, I dare not speak a word.   95
KING
  Nor I, and yet methinks I should command;
  But seeing I cannot, I'll entreat for him:
  My lord, if you will let my uncle live
  I will requite it when I come to age.
MORTIMER JUNIOR
  'Tis for your highness' good, and for the realm's;   100
  How often shall I bid you bear him hence?
KENT
  Art thou king, must I die at thy command?
MORTIMER JUNIOR
  At our command; once more away with him.
KENT
  Let me but stay and speak, I will not go;
  Either my brother or his son is king,   105
  And none of both them thirst for Edmund's blood.
  And therefore, soldiers, whither will you hale me?

They hale EDMUND EARL OF KENT *away, and carry him to be
beheaded*

KING
  What safety may I look for at his hands
  If that my uncle shall be murthered thus?
QUEEN
  Fear not, sweet boy, I'll guard thee from thy foes;   110
  Had Edmund lived, he would have sought thy death.
  Come, son, we'll ride ahunting in the park.
KING
  And shall my uncle Edmund ride with us?
QUEEN
  He is a traitor, think not on him; come.   [*Exeunt*]

[Act V, Scene v]

Enter MATREVIS *and* GURNEY

MATREVIS
 Gurney, I wonder the king dies not,
 Being in a vault up to the knees in water,
 To which the channels of the castle run,
 From whence a damp continually ariseth,
 That were enough to poison any man,   5
 Much more a king brought up so tenderly.
GURNEY
 And so do I, Matrevis; yesternight
 I opened but the door to throw him meat
 And I was almost stifled with the savour.
MATREVIS
 He hath a body able to endure   10
 More than we can inflict and therefore now
 Let us assail his mind another while.
GURNEY
 Send for him out thence and I will anger him.
MATREVIS
 But stay, who's this?

Enter LIGHTBORN [*bearing a letter*]

LIGHTBORN   My lord Protector greets you.
GURNEY
 What's here? I know not how to conster it.   15

---

15 *conster* interpret, construe

---

 1 *I wonder the king dies not.* The endurance of the king in face of physical
  sufferings before which his coarse persecutors flinch, is the final and
  redeeming sign of his regality; it materially shifts the tone of the concluding scenes.
 10 *He hath a body able to endure . . .* If Levin's conjecture has substance
  that Lightborn is demonic (see Note to V. iv, 21) this whole passage in
  temper and phraseology recalls the 'sifting' of the Old Man in *Doctor
  Faustus*. In Scene xviii Faustus asks Mephistophiles that the Old Man
  be tormented 'with greatest torment that our hell affords', to which
  Mephistophiles replies in words that recall Matrevis here:

    His faith is great; I cannot touch his soul;
    But what I may afflict his body with
    I will attempt, which is but little worth.

MATREVIS

    Gurney, it was left unpointed for the nonce;
    '*Edwardum occidere nolite timere*',
    That's his meaning.

LIGHTBORN

    Know you this token? I must have the king.

MATREVIS

    Ay, stay awhile, thou shalt have answer straight.   20
    [*Aside*] This villain's sent to make away the king.

GURNEY

    [*Aside*] I thought as much.

MATREVIS   And when the murder's done,
    See how he must be handled for his labour,
    Pereat iste. Let him have the king;
    What else? here are the keys, this is the lake;   25
    [*To* LIGHTBORN] Do as you are commanded by my lord.

LIGHTBORN

    I know what I must do, get you away,
    Yet be not far off, I shall need your help;
    See that in the next room I have a fire,
    And get me a spit and let it be red-hot.   30

MATREVIS

    Very well.

GURNEY

    Need you anything besides?

LIGHTBORN

    What else? a table and a featherbed.

GURNEY

    That's all?

LIGHTBORN

    Ay, ay, so when I call you, bring it in.   35

MATREVIS

    Fear not you that.

GURNEY

    Here's a light to go into the dungeon.

---

16 *for the nonce* expressly
24 *Pereat iste* let him die   25 *lake* dungeon

---

30 *get me a spit.* For the 'propriety' of King Edward's end, see Introduction, p. xxi. Marlowe treats the whole incident with great restraint
though his source is explicit: 'they kept him downe, and withall put into
his fundament an horne, and through the same they thrust up into his
bodie a hote spitte . . . so as no appearance of any wounds or hurt out-
wardie might be once perceyved'.

LIGHTBORN
    So now must I about this gear; ne'er was there any
    So finely handled as this king shall be;
    Foh! here's a place indeed with all my heart!   40
EDWARD
    Who's there, what light is that, wherefore comest thou?
LIGHTBORN
    To comfort you and bring you joyful news.
EDWARD
    Small comfort finds poor Edward in thy looks;
    Villain, I know thou comest to murther me.
LIGHTBORN
    To murther you my most gracious lord?   45
    Far is it from my heart to do you harm;
    The queen sent me to see how you were used,
    For she relents at this your misery.
    And what eyes can refrain from shedding tears
    To see a king in this most piteous state?   50
EDWARD
    Weep'st thou already? list awhile to me
    And then thy heart, were it as Gurney's is,
    Or as Matrevis', hewn from the Caucasus,
    Yet will it melt ere I have done my tale.
    This dungeon where they keep me is the sink   55
    Wherein the filth of all the castle falls.
LIGHTBORN
    Oh villains!
EDWARD
    And there in mire and puddle have I stood
    This ten days' space, and lest that I should sleep,
    One plays continually upon a drum;   60
    They give me bread and water being a king,
    So that for want of sleep and sustenance
    My mind's distempered and my body's numbed,
    And whether I have limbs or no I know not;
    Oh would my blood dropped out from every vein   65
    As doth this water from my tattered robes;
    Tell Isabel the queen, I looked not thus
    When for her sake I ran at tilt in France
    And there unhorsed the Duke of Cleremont.
LIGHTBORN
    Oh speak no more, my lord, this breaks my heart!   70
    Lie on this bed and rest yourself awhile.

EDWARD

These looks of thine can harbour nought but death.
I see my tragedy written in thy brows;
Yet stay awhile, forbear thy bloody hand
And let me see the stroke before it comes   75
That even then when I shall lose my life
My mind may be more steadfast on my God.

LIGHTBORN

What means your highness to mistrust me thus?

EDWARD

What means thou to dissemble with me thus?

LIGHTBORN

These hands were never stained with innocent blood   80
Nor shall they now be tainted with a king's.

EDWARD

Forgive my thought for having such a thought;
One jewel have I left, receive thou this.
Still fear I, and I know not what's the cause,
But every joint shakes as I give it thee.   85
Oh if thou harbourest murther in thy heart,
Let this gift change thy mind and save thy soul;
Know that I am a king; oh, at that name
I feel a hell of grief; where is my crown?
Gone, gone! and do I remain alive?   90

LIGHTBORN

You're overwatched, my lord, lie down and rest.

EDWARD

But that grief keeps me waking, I should sleep,
For not these ten days have these eyes'-lids closed;
Now as I speak they fall, and yet with fear
Open again; Oh wherefore sit'st thou here?   95

LIGHTBORN

If you mistrust me, I'll be gone, my lord.

EDWARD

No, no, for if thou meanest to murther me,
Thou wilt return again, and therefore stay.

LIGHTBORN

[*Aside*] He sleeps.

EDWARD

Oh let me not die; yet stay, oh stay awhile.   100

73 *tragedy* final end

---

77 *My mind may be more steadfast on my God.* Edward wishes to make in
every way 'a good end', in clear mind and knowing his moment of death.

LIGHTBORN
  How now, my lord?
EDWARD
  Something still buzzeth in mine ears,
  And tells me if I sleep I never wake;
  This fear is that which makes me tremble thus
  And therefore tell me, wherefore art thou come?   105
LIGHTBORN
  To rid thee of thy life; Matrevis, come.
EDWARD
  I am too weak and feeble to resist;
  Assist me, sweet God, and receive my soul.
LIGHTBORN
  Run for the table.
EDWARD
  Oh spare me, or dispatch me in a trice.   110
LIGHTBORN
  So, lay the table down, and stamp on it,
  But not too hard, lest that you bruise his body.
MATREVIS
  I fear me that this cry will raise the town,
  And therefore let us take horse and away.
LIGHTBORN
  Tell me first, was it not bravely done?   115
GURNEY
  Excellent well; take this for thy reward.

          [*Then* GURNEY *stabs* LIGHTBORN]

  Come let us cast the body in the moat
  And bear the king's to Mortimer our lord.
  Away!   [*Exeunt*]

[Act V, Scene vi]

Enter MORTIMER JUNIOR *and* MATREVIS

MORTIMER JUNIOR
  Is't done, Matrevis, and the murtherer dead?
MATREVIS
  Ay my good lord, I would it were undone.

110 *dispatch me in a trice.* The implied stage directions, the preparations in
    another room, probably suggest the murder, heard but not seen, behind
    the arras of a stage pavilion or 'inner stage'. Hence the stress upon the
    sound of death, Edward's cry (l. 113) which is especially noted in the
    Chronicle source: 'His crie did move many . . . to compassion'.

MORTIMER JUNIOR
  Matrevis, if thou now growest penitent
  I'll be thy ghostly father; therefore choose
  Whether thou wilt be secret in this   5
  Or else die by the hand of Mortimer.
MATREVIS
  Gurney, my lord, is fled, and will I fear
  Betray us both, therefore let me fly.
MORTIMER JUNIOR
  Fly to the savages.
MATREVIS
  I humbly thank your honour.   [*Exit*]   10
MORTIMER JUNIOR
  As for myself, I stand as Jove's huge tree,
  And others are but shrubs compared to me,
  All tremble at my name, and I fear none,
  Let's see who dare impeach me for his death?

              [*Enter the* QUEEN]

QUEEN
  Ah Mortimer, the king my son hath news   15
  His father's dead and we have murdered him.
MORTIMER JUNIOR
  What if he have? the king is yet a child.
QUEEN
  Ay, ay, but he tears his hair and wrings his hands,
  And vows to be revenged upon us both;
  Into the council chamber he is gone   20
  To crave the aid and succour of his peers;
  Ay me! see where he comes and they with him;
  Now Mortimer, begins our tragedy.

       Enter the KING, *with the* LORDS

---

4 *ghostly father* confessor (before his death)
23 *tragedy* tragic *dénouement* (cf. V. v, 73 above)

9–10 *Fly to the savages* / *I humbly thank your honour.* The dramatic irony
  now shifts. Like the murderers of Richard II, Matrevis and Gurney
  are disowned as mere instruments. This passage between Mortimer and
  Matrevis ironically places Mortimer's court beneath the savages.
11–23 *I stand as Jove's huge tree . . . Now Mortimer, begins our tragedy.*
  Marlowe requires only fourteen lines to manipulate a dramatic reversal
  from God-like security ('Jove's huge tree') to dereliction ('our tragedy')
  which in historic time took three years, from 1327 to 1330.

LORDS
Fear not, my lord, know that you are a king.
KING
Vil!ain.   25
MORTIMER JUNIOR
How now, my lord?
KING
Think not that I am frighted with thy words;
My father's murdered through thy treachery,
And thou shalt die and on his mournful hearse
Thy hateful and accursed head shall lie,   30
To witness to the world, that by thy means
His kingly body was too soon interred.
QUEEN
Weep not, sweet son.
KING
Forbid not me to weep, he was my father,
And had you loved him half so well as I,   35
You could not bear his death thus patiently;
But you, I fear, conspired with Mortimer.
LORDS
Why speak you not unto my lord the king?
MORTIMER JUNIOR
Because I think scorn to be accused;
Who is the man dare say I murdered him?   40
KING
Traitor, in me my loving father speaks
And plainly saith 'twas thou that murderedst him.
MORTIMER JUNIOR
But hath your grace no other proof than this?
KING
Yes, if this be the hand of Mortimer.
                    [*Shows letter to* MORTIMER]
MORTIMER JUNIOR
False Gurney hath betrayed me and himself.   45
QUEEN
I feared as much; murther cannot be hid.
MORTIMER JUNIOR
'Tis my hand; what gather you by this?
KING
That thither thou didst send a murtherer.

41 *Traitor, in me my loving father speaks.* Marlowe carefully withholds this
   final show of authority in the young prince until, at this point, at the
   death of his father, he is king in legal fact.

MORTIMER JUNIOR
What murtherer? bring forth the man I sent.
KING
Ah Mortimer, thou knowest that he is slain   50
And so shalt thou be too; why stays he here?
Bring him unto a hurdle, drag him forth,
Hang him I say, and set his quarters up,
But bring his head back presently to me.
QUEEN
For my sake, sweet son, pity Mortimer.   55
MORTIMER JUNIOR
Madam, entreat not, I will rather die,
Than sue for life unto a paltry boy.
KING
Hence with the traitor, with the murderer.
MORTIMER JUNIOR
Base fortune, now I see, that in thy wheel
There is a point to which when men aspire   60
They tumble headlong down; that point I touched
And seeing there was no place to mount up higher
Why should I grieve at my declining fall?
Farewell, fair queen, weep not for Mortimer
That scorns the world and as a traveller   65
Goes to discover countries yet unknown.
KING
What, suffer you the traitor to delay?
                              [MORTIMER *taken away*]
QUEEN
As thou receivedst thy life from me,
Spill not the blood of gentle Mortimer.
KING
This argues that you spilt my father's blood,   70
Else would you not entreat for Mortimer.
QUEEN
I spill his blood? no.
KING
Ay, madam, you, for so the rumour runs.
QUEEN
That rumour is untrue; for loving thee
Is this report raised on poor Isabel.   75

---

59 *Base fortune, now I see* . . . Mortimer reaches the same insight concerning fortune's way with men as the earlier heroes of Marlowe.

KING
    I do not think her so unnatural.
LORDS
    My lord, I fear me it will prove too true.
KING
    Mother, you are suspected for his death,
    And therefore we commit you to the Tower,
    Till further trial may be made thereof;   80
    If you be guilty, though I be your son,
    Think not to find me slack or pitiful.
QUEEN
    Nay, to my death, for too long have I lived
    Whenas my son thinks to abridge my days.
KING
    Away with her, her words enforce these tears   85
    And I shall pity her if she speak again.
QUEEN
    Shall I not mourn for my beloved lord?
    And with the rest accompany him to his grave.
LORDS
    Thus, madam, 'tis the king's will you shall hence.
QUEEN
    He hath forgotten me, stay, I am his mother.   90
LORDS
    That boots not, therefore, gentle madam, go.
QUEEN
    Then come sweet death and rid me of this grief.

                    [*Enter a* LORD]
LORDS
    My lord, here is the head of Mortimer.
KING
    Go fetch my father's hearse where it shall lie
    And bring my funeral robes. Accursed head,   95
    Could I have ruled thee then as I do now
    Thou hadst not hatched this monstrous treachery.
    Here comes the hearse, help me to mourn, my lords.
    Sweet father, here unto thy murdered ghost
    I offer up this wicked traitor's head   100
    And let these tears distilling from mine eyes
    Be witness of my grief and innocency.   [*Exeunt*]

                    FINIS

Printed in Great Britain by
The Garden City Press Limited
Letchworth Hertfordshire